SECOND PRINTING: 2007

ISBN (old school) 0-9777665-2-7
ISBN (new school) 978-0-9777665-2-9

Manufactured in the United States of America by the tolerant people at
Morris Publishing.
Morrispublishing.com

Published by The Deadxstop Publishing Company.
Contact us at: deadxstop@aol.com

Cover design by Jean-Paul Frijns.
jeanpaul@valueofstrength.com
Interior page layout by Kelly Gheesling.
Sweet author pictures by Nicole Vurusic.
Edited by Sara Appino and Brooke Matelis.

"A Picture is Worth A Thousand Words...Most of them Lies" was titled by Sandra L. Howley in a
contest sponsored by Buzznet.com

NOTE: This is a work of non-fiction. While the author took every opportunity to ensure the
stories included were 100% on the up and up, he is flawed and forgetful just like you. In some
cases, dialogue from twenty years ago may not be entirely accurate but just know that the author
went above and beyond to contact the people involved to verify every aspect of the story. All
names, characters and incidents are real, even if the people involved deny they ever happened,
which we wouldn't entirely blame them for.

Commence lurking:

Myspace.com/askheychris
Myspace.com/thedeadxstoppublishingcompany
Askheychris.com
Deadxstop.buzznet.com
Askheychris.livejournal.com

For my first hero.

Foreword

୫ଠଝ

"I realized that either I was crazy or the world was crazy; and I picked on the world. And of course I was right." – Jack Kerouac

As soon as the last word of this quote rolled off the silent-tongue of my inner monologue, the above excerpt (parted from the lips of a life-hungry and road-weary poet) struck a chord somewhere deep inside. It resonated in a place that is rarely moved, and when it is, it is usually only music that proves able to move it. Music, to me at least, is one of the few mediums that seems to be able to accomplish something that words often fall short of. A chorus of guitars can haunt your dreams, a bass line can give you the chills, and a gut-wrenching lyric thrust from the lungs of someone who means it can break your heart. I'm guilty of relying solely on music for these experiences, but sometimes someone like Kerouac comes along and gives guitar riffs a serious run for their money...

This time Christopher Gutierrez came along. He stepped up to the plate and brought the fickle crowd that lives in my head to their feet. His memoirs inspire as good as the best hardcore song you ever heard, maybe better. Today's generation seems to have hijacked the superficial parts of what punk and hardcore started, and they left the meaning, the substance, and the guts behind. Fret not, because you'll find those missing guts between these pages. Every generation has a voice, and one day I'm sure that a panel of pop-culture experts will choose one for my generation. But it will be too late for me, because I've already found one. He is the father of the words you are about to inhale. They are born from the angst, the joy, the pain, the laughter, the reality, and the dreams of his own life; A Life Deliberate. Words can be as volatile as a Molotov cocktail, especially when they are as sincere as these, as those words document our purpose in life and how important it is to chase that purpose to the ends of the earth, or at least to the ends of the internet.

- Timothy McIlrath, Rise Against

"Rock bottom is a beautiful start."

- Modern Life Is War, "Destination: Death or Better Days."

Contents

An Introduction

ഔ

Sometimes I find it difficult to convey the warmth I have in my chest. Ironic, because it is the only thing that is real. The words, the passion, the honesty. This is genuine and therefore extremely difficult. Truth and love and appreciation make us vulnerable, and my goal is to ultimately be as vulnerable as I can tolerate, and then some. Because the freedom we all search for isn't within someone else, or a paycheck, or a comfortable lover. That freedom lies in our heads and our hearts and our legs that carry us and our fingers that type with sincerity and conviction. And I want to be free. I want to let it all go; the animosity and the hate and the villainy and the apathy and the black spots on my brain. I want to breathe in the good and exhale the abuse and fights and the words that don't match the actions. I want to live deliberate, so that every ounce of dirty and filthy energy I take from this world is shaken and stirred in this head and heart and returned back to your eyes and ears in the most purified and genuine form I have the courage to deliver: These words.

I am simply a boy letting go of the ugly through words and actions. And you are my unfortunate audience.

It is terrifying. While I smile and dance and sing and steal, every day is a new day. Every day is a new beginning because I refuse to let the horror of my past control the direction or the intensity of my love.

And those are the memories that push me.

And yours are the ears and eyes and hugs and "thank yous" that guide me.

And yours is the attention that motivates me.

And yours are the confessions that captivate me.

Today, like tomorrow and the day after, is a new day.

A. New. Day.

To start again. To become the people we always wanted to be. To take the first step to really live. To stick our necks out. To breathe out the shame. To eat our dessert first. To not give in to our petty fears. Because every single day the sun shines on <u>us</u>. It bows to each and every one of us. And the problem is that instead of seeing it as our ally, we see it as our oppressor. And it is that misconception that has been robbing us of our life since we were old enough to cry out for what we have desired.

Tomorrow your life will be a day shorter. You will have one less day to expose your heart and give yourself the opportunity to let the bad out in order to make room for the good. You will have one less day to make your life an exceptional life.

And while I'm still running my uphill battle against the wind, I haven't given up yet. Every day I try to make the words I speak in her ear on those dark and cold nights and the words I type on this old and worn out keyboard mirror my actions and the love I send out. And that is the hard part. But that is why I do it, not only because it is hard but because it is damn near impossible.

We Are the Dirt Poets

ॐ

Standing there in the aisle I couldn't decide which ones to pick. Green with white stitching would clearly increase the odds of random arm punches and back-of-the-neck slaps from the older and much larger kids.

Brown would have to do. I grabbed the shoes off of the shelf. They were plastic and the tag read $9.99. I held them in front of me under the yellow lighting of the clearance section. They were ugly and I knew it, but they would help me blend and melt into the white cinderblock walls of seventh grade. One part of me was thankful that I was making progress towards fitting in, because I was moving towards that "Miami Vice" look that was deemed cool that year.

These shoes were also one more way to avoid the hairy knuckles of the imposing wrestlers looking for any reason to stab me in the back with something sharp, the weapon of choice was a multicolored push pin, stolen from the woodshop bulletin board.

Placed in-between their middle and ring fingers the pins were concealed just enough in the palm to be undetected by hall monitors, but protruded just enough to make it through whatever thin t-shirt I happened to be wearing

Walking back to my mother's shopping cart filled with potted plants and the many pairs of pleated slacks I talked her into buying for me, I placed the brown boat shoes into the cart

1

with a bit of hesitation. It felt wrong. I felt like I was lying to myself, but my overwhelming sense of self-preservation managed to justify the purchase.

The cool kids who had girlfriends and told stories of "getting to third base" wore boat shoes. I never saw anyone with tight rolled slacks, boat shoes, and polo shirts get the shit beat out of them. They were always the hatchet men, the wrestlers, the tough guys. The kind of guys small, skinny, and girly kids like me prayed we could be friends with, and so desperately wished we could become. I figured that maybe if I emulated their swag, I could have a piece of that bulletproof life.

I hated their music, their lack of reasoning, and their sense of style. I knew they would look back in ten years and regret their pleated French-rolled slacks and massive, metal, mall hair. They were ugly. Their feathered hair and their Duran Duran dance steps made me gag, and I so desperately wanted to hang onto break dancing which had just been deemed "out" and "uncool" by everyone else. But break dancing made me feel alive. Sure, I may have embarrassed myself on the cardboard like a flailing idiot, but goddamn I loved the parachute pants, fingerless gloves, beats, and the socially conscious lyrics of the likes of Grandmaster Flash. Even if I didn't know about life in the ghetto, I knew they were speaking about real life, not this glossy dance pop that ruled the popular radio stations.

But now, in order to avoid punches to the spine and being called a "faggot", I was walking behind a shopping cart carrying a plastic pair of brown boat shoes. Similar to the kind the bullies wore, only cheaper and shittier. I wanted to be able to hold my head up and to walk into the gym locker room without fear, just like the assholes who pushed me around for having the same "pussyboy" unfashionable haircut since 4th grade, and just like the mindless kids who danced with wide eyes and gleaming white smiles to OMD's "If You Leave…" song during the school dances in the gym. I wanted to be like them. -Not in their hateful and meat-headed ways, but to be untouchable. To be noticed.

I walked alongside the cart and watched as my mother took the shoes and placed them on the checkout counter. The checkout lady rang up the shoes, placed them in a bag, and handed them to me with a smile.

"Thank you," I responded.

But I didn't feel good about the victory. They were merely a ten-dollar investment to hopefully gain me entry into a clique I really didn't want to be a part of in the first place. I knew I was a fraud. See, I wanted to be "like" them, not "part of" them. I wanted to walk the halls free of harassment like they did. I wanted to sit at the "cool kids" table. I wanted to be referred to as the "A squad". I wanted an identity. I wanted to feel qualified in the eyes of my peers.

Because I didn't in my own mirror at home.

I had made one fatal mistake, I assumed their lack of creativity and individuality was indicative of their inability to smell a fraud. I was proven wrong in first period math the next day.

"Ah ha," cried out the jock who had an affinity for punching my kidneys. "Look at his plastic shoes!"

"See, I told you he wants to try and fit in," his friend who sat in the desk next to him yelled out.

I wanted to die. Every single person in the class stared at me in silence while the laughing echoed throughout the room. Every girl I had a crush on, every one of my "friends", they sat and watched me take it.

I walked to my desk and sat down. Their cackling made me wince and I held in the tears. I felt my face throb with embarrassment. I gripped the sides of my desk in anger. I wanted to stand up and yell, "I DID THIS SO YOU WOULD LIKE ME!"

But they kept laughing and I kept my eyes on the door, praying that the teacher would walk in so the heaviness in the room would fade. I stared out the window and made an attempt to control my heaving and fluttering lungs.

It felt like days before the door opened and the teacher came in and told everyone to settle down. It was a simple day like any other. One minute in the lifetime of thirty people that has been forgotten by everyone involved...everyone but me. I held on to that moment.

In that moment, I wanted to throw the shoes out the window. I wanted to cry out, "ALL I WANT IS TO BE LIKE YOU!"

But I didn't.

I sat there and I took it. And while I didn't defend myself...I also didn't run, nor did I let the tears fall. Because they were watching. They saw the red eyes and they kept looking back as the teacher scribbled words on the blackboard. Whispering back and forth to each other, they covered their mouths and giggled, and I repeated over and over in my head, "Do not fall. Please, dear God do not let these tears fall from my eyes."

And they didn't.

And I never forgot that moment, because somewhere in there, I felt the importance.

It's like the first time you hear that one song that is so huge and epic that you have to rush home and play it on your stereo. While you're incapable of understanding the gravity of that moment, the volumes pass through your ears and boom and rebound in your skull. You can feel there is something grand and epic going on, and you can't wait to spend every waking minute trying to comprehend the beauty and complexity, but you're so frustrated because your little heart still has its training wheels and lacks the capacity to hold or understand the overwhelming significance of the moment.

Yes, me sitting in that desk was that epic moment because

I.

Didn't.

Run.

It was ironic that on the way home that day, the shoes began to fall apart. The small metal rings on the sides that held in the purportedly fashionable laces came loose and stuck out like jagged little barbs. As I walked down the street they rubbed up against my ankles. I hated those shoes and couldn't wait to throw them out the minute I walked through the door. In all of my youthful exuberance, I ran half way home. When I eventually ran through the door to throw them in the trash, I reached down and noticed that the rings had cut small gashes into my ankles. I don't scar easily. And almost twenty years later, those scars are still visible.

That night, while I lay in bed, I tried to figure out why that moment felt so poignant.

It was my baptism into the 'I won't be beat', spirit.

It was my first bite of self-confidence.

It was my first step into becoming an individual. It was the moment when a boy becomes a man, and it was my first unaided step into recognizing the beauty that is my inner strength. This was true independence and faith and it was my introduction to the glow of my heart.

The next day, I walked into school wearing what I felt most comfortable in, ripped up skater gear, and, as if on cue, the bullies laughed. Oh, it still hurt, and while my face burned red, I noticed my eyes didn't water. The day after that, they laughed and my faced burned less, and the day after that my face didn't burn at all.

While I may have only been in 7th grade, and possessed the confidence of a newborn duck, I realized that if I ever wanted to move that mountain of self-doubt out of my heart, I had to do it one rock at a time. Each day after that, when I walked into class and I didn't cry or feel embarrassed, my confidence grew, and that mountain got smaller.

Later that year, the last day before Christmas vacation, at the end of fifth period literature, my friend Billy called me over to his desk. "Dude, listen to this," he said handing me a pair of headphones.

"Ahh!" I shouted. "What is all this screamy stuff? This sucks!"

"Dude," he said. Clearly I had ruffled his feathers. "Dude, this is the Sex Pistols, they're like totally punk rock."

"Well, it sounds like a mess to me."

I hated it. It wasn't upbeat and catchy, nor could I distinguish the lyrics, but there was something in the screaming, something I couldn't figure out, something that, even though I couldn't make out the words, reverberated in my head. Something in that music shook me and knocked me around in a good way, like the ten seconds after you step off of a carnival tilt-a-whirl.

That vacation, I was handed a few tapes of some of the more popular punk rock bands at the time, and they shook me as well.

They screamed like the midnight burnout parties the drunken potheads across the street would throw on the weekends...but not exactly in the same way. There was an intensity and direction with this new music. I didn't want, I NEEDED to know more about it. It wasn't a word or a phrase or a song that snagged my heart. It was the passion with which it was being screamed. It was true art. It was the first real threat I had ever heard. It was the words I could not yet speak. It was danger and desire and fury. It was all that, and it was a dagger in the back of mediocrity and insincerity. It put the breath in my lungs and gave me a direction in which to scream. So I listened and I learned and I grew and I fell in love for the first time.

The music screamed into my ears and into my heart the words that described that moment in 7th grade Math class when I refused to let the tears fall. That thing, that thing that I never spoke of but kept me awake at night. THAT was what they screamed of. They yelled about finding the glory in those hot and embarrassed faces of 7th grade. They didn't speak about love and loss and all that boring pretty-boy pop the radio preached, they yelled real romance and made NOT fitting in a glorious feeling. To not only hold on to what makes you YOU, but to "celebrate" it. .

That year, I walked into school looking as ridiculous as possible. I donned everything from green Mohawks, to safety pins and rips in my clothes, to combat boots and spiked collars. I wanted the pretty kids to see that their status in the 7th grade pecking order was hollow and built upon hypocrisy and conformity.

I wanted to stand up and make them see that I wasn't part of them, that I would never try to be and that I would be proud of the of genuine hearts that I considered true friends.

What I looked for in their cliques and parties and lunchroom tables I had found in myself, without their help, and without anyone else. That I didn't want any part of their club, so I made my own.

I realized that their bullying and exclusionary tactics were simply a result of their inability to look at their own reflection without flinching.

Every, "faggot" and "pussy" that fell from their lips boldly illustrated their lack of self-worth and screamed insecurity.

I looked upon those kids with pity, I eventually saw them as feeble and powerless and I never again looked to their table with envious eyes.

So when this kid looked in the mirror he now saw a different boy. Staring back at him he saw merit, worth and true love for the first time. It was the beginning of a long and trying and extraordinary journey of self-discovery. I was on a momentous yet unwavering pilgrimage to meet the man who was at the helm of this heart.

And as daunting and intimidating as this journey was going to be, I was determined to meet that man and make my peace. So that one day I could look in the mirror, and with all the confidence of every man that has ever walked this planet, say to myself, "I believe in you."

The New Guard

શ્ચિલ્સ

The twelve of us sat on a tree that had fallen across the river. Each of us were covered head to toe in camouflage with BB guns strapped across our backs; we were taking a break from playing war in the forest that was adjacent to our neighborhood. Well, I suppose it wasn't so much "playing war" as it was "designing the most perfect of fortifications from the impending Russian invasion." See, this was the 80s and in the 80s there were three main threats to everyone who lived and breathed on American soil.

The first threat was that each and every last kid under the age of twelve would be the target of a kidnapping plot. I don't know what it was, but every kid was being abducted in the 80s. What with the barrage of after-school specials and made-for-TV movies that were shown to us in school on a monthly basis, one would have thought there were roving bands of masked villains in vans lurking around every corner to steal us and whisk us away to some dark and dank basement where we would be tied to a chair and gagged while our tormentors played phone tag with the police and our parents over the ransom drop spot. Unfortunately, the truth was that after our funerals, our lower-middle-class, single parents probably would have welcomed the fact that they would no longer have to clean our dirty foot prints from their aging shag carpets or worry about how they were going to raise the money to buy the new hot BMX bike that we all so desperately needed to look cool. We were children of the 80s so naturally we were greedy, regardless of income, class, or tax bracket.

The second issue that plagued our communities was AIDS. Again, with the TV movies and 20/20 specials, EVERYONE was convinced we were doomed to suffer a life of AIDS. There were AIDS ridden hypodermic needles in every trashcan, on every park bench, and hidden deep in our mailboxes. At one point, our class was told by our panic-ridden 5th grade teacher, "You kids will be lucky to see 50. At the rate AIDS is killing everyone, you may be one of the last generation on this planet." I thought about how awesome that would be: Me, one of the last representatives of the entire race. I thought about the chaos and turmoil it would throw the world into; stealing, looting, burning buildings, breaking windows...yeah, it would be awesome. I was a troubled and bored kid from a broken home, and do you know what troubled and bored kids from broken homes aspire to accomplish? Stealing, looting, burning buildings, and breaking windows. -I couldn't WAIT for Armageddon.

Which leads us to our third plague of the 80s; nuclear war. During the 80s, I saw two pivotal movies at the local movie theater that instilled the McCarthy era "Red Scare" into the back of my brain: "Red Dawn" and "Back to the Future." While the story in "Back to the Future" focused more on time travel and the hijinx that ensued, at our young age we were intelligent enough to read between the lines and see the message our government was sending: The Libyans wanted nothing more than to secure plutonium to make a nuclear bomb to drop down and cripple the suburbs of Chicago, thereby securing an entrance way for an impending invasion. Which leads us to "Red Dawn." In "Red Dawn" we learned that it was the communist backed army of Afghanistan that came parachuting out of the sky to invade our land, steal our women, and take away our Ataris. They didn't attack the coasts or the major cities, they came right into an unsuspecting small town in Colorado, and if we took anything away from these cinematic masterpieces it was to be prepared and ready our town for World War III. If we heard a low flying helicopter, it was the evil Russians. If we saw a seemingly suspicious jet in the sky, it was those damn commie Cubans.

We wouldn't sit complacent like our ex-hippy parents who sold out their ideals and chopped off their balls in lieu of manicured lawns, mini-vans and Jazzercise classes. We were the new guard, raised on "Rambo" and "Iron Eagle" and "Missing in Action" movies. We loved ninjas, Cinemax After-Dark programming, and playing war, and we would be damned if any dirty Communist would get their hands on our Def Leppard tapes. Even if we didn't have a clue what a Communist government's ideals were, shit, we figured if it wasn't good enough for the Wolverines in "Red Dawn" then it wasn't good enough for us, goddamnit.

That afternoon, twelve of us sat on that fallen tree above a rushing river with a serious undercurrent that had recently taken the life of a tough 18 year-old metal head in an Iron Maiden t-shirt. And in 1984, an Iron Maiden t-shirt made you a tough hoodlum and if a tough burn-out could be swept away and killed by a river, we knew we had to gather as many kids in the neighborhood and test their "pussy factor" to see if they could hang with us once the Russians came. We swung our feet over the edge and we joked around about each other's mothers, because that's what you did when you were in fourth grade. We thought of new defense plans for the fortification of our "base", which was really nothing more than a torn down wooden fence that we shoved up a tree. Plans for the tiger pit trap that we began digging on a popular trail that ran uncomfortably close to our headquarters had to be scrapped due to the fact that it's super fucking hard for an adult to dig a six foot hole in the ground, let alone a rag-tag group of little kids armed with their mother's gardening shovels. We had other plans, like a network of poison tipped blow guns strategically hidden in bushes, and even if we didn't know where to get poison to arm the darts, we could certainly perforate the enemy with hundreds of our mothers tiny sewing needles. Then there was the ever-popular barbed wire trap. We had planned to string barbed wire from tree to tree in a sort of maze so that if we had to retreat we could run a certain pattern through the trees and our unsuspecting pursuers wouldn't have the advance knowledge of the safe route through the barbed wire forest, and they would be ensnarled and left to bleed to death while their comrades stood by and watched helplessly. In reality, the only barbed wire we could find was from a nearby abandoned farm, and with the limited supply of fifty-year-old rusted barbed wire we effortlessly snapped off with the flick of the wrist, the most we could have hoped for was to be chased by an army of hemophiliacs who, when scratched, would have bled to death in maybe 4 to 5 years.

Yeah, we had plans all right. We would have our own band of Wolverines. Twelve kids from 3rd to 6th grade who had everything they needed to defeat an invading army of godless savages who wanted nothing more than to take away our liberty. We were to be heroes. And while our parents made fun of us when we painted our faces to resemble the camouflage outfits we wore, we knew in the back of our minds that the day would come when we would be paraded through the streets of our town to a tickertape parade and take our rightful place in the community as nobility and statesmen. We were young, but we had ideals. We knew we had to pick up the slack for our parents and that day, on that log, between the mom jokes and our improvised MacGyver-like booby trap planning we were unequaled and untouchable.

I looked over at my friend Jerry and said, "Dude, this is the spot where that burn-out kid who lived up the street from me fell in and drowned."

Looking from me to the water Jerry said surprisingly, "No way."

"Yeah," I said matter-of-factly. "And that dude was big and tough and he couldn't fight the undertow. Imagine if we fell in."

Joking he looked over at me and feigned like he was going to throw me in. I pretended to panic, then laughed. We sat back, I took off my army green field pack and threw open the flap. Digging around on the inside I pulled out one of my mother's "famous" condiment sandwiches: lettuce, mustard, and American cheese on white bread. I unwrapped the sandwich, looked down at the river that glittered like gold from the overhead sun, and took a bite. I stopped chewing when I heard a very distinct sound in the distance. It was far away but progressively got louder.

"Dude, do you hear that?" Jerry said.

"Yeah, what is that noise?" I responded.

"Dude it sounds like..." he paused.

"AIR RAID SIRENS!" We seemed to yell in unison.

I clearly remember my eye instantaneously filling with the panic-filled tears of the Armageddon. I looked over to the other kids who leapt to their feet on the fallen tree and began putting one foot in front of the other like ants on a leaf making a desperate dash to safe ground. I put both my hands on the log, pushed myself up to my feet, and turned to run; only there was a line of terrified and watery-eyed kids in front of me. I looked around to everyone on either side and yelled, "RUN! HURRY! RUN!"

We all knew what was coming: The bombs.

I couldn't take it anymore; it was every man for himself.

In my haste I went to push Jerry out of the way and inadvertently missed my footing and slipped backward.

Slow motion.

I took a deep breath and held it.

I looked up at the clear blue sky and saw the sun.

Then, I saw black.

I was underwater, fighting for my life in the river that had recently killed a local tough-ass bully, worst of all, I couldn't swim.

In my horror I screamed out all of my air and instantly breathed in a lungful of brown and murky water. I threw my arms about in a fury, clawing at the water, desperately trying to push it out of my way to the surface. I emerged and screamed out like I was on fire. I could see the scatter of scared little men running and falling haphazardly through the forest. I could hear someone crying for his mother.

Surprisingly, I bobbed up and down, held afloat by the many layers of heavy camouflage clothing that trapped in the air. I was being taken down stream but I was making slow progress through the water towards the edge. My lungs were now paralyzed by the fear of being sucked under by the impending undertow and the fact that any help I would have had were now literally peeing in their pants and sprinting out of the woods back to the shelter of their houses.

This wasn't the way it was supposed to end, heroes didn't drown while eating condiment sandwiches!

This was it; I was going to die. That was, until I stretched out my legs and could feel the mud underneath my feet. I stood straight up and the water was only up to my chest.

Luckily, that summer was particularly dry thereby lowering the water level and making it possible for this lame duck of a swimmer to walk effortlessly through the rushing water to the shore. I slipped and fell face first into the shallow end of the river. On my hands and knees, I climbed up the muddy riverbank, tore off my backpack, and immediately took off running in the direction of my retreating friends. Fortunately I was fast and caught up to them in a matter of minutes.

"Are we going to die?" Kevin, the youngest of our group screamed, while running and looking back over his shoulder.

"Man, I don't know," I said coughing water out of my lungs, "I've heard those sirens before on that movie 'Threads'."

"Threads," like its counterpart, "The Day After" was one of those 80s movies designed to put the fear of God into the viewer by boldly illustrating in all of its gory detail the effect the blast of a nuclear bomb would have on our country. According to those movies, either our skin would melt from our bones, or as a result of the fallout radiation we could expect to die a slow, cancer-filled, agonizing death. I place the blame squarely upon these two movies for the Pavlovian response connection between that distinct warning from those sirens and an incoming missile strike.

Our little legs and our panting lungs that felt as if they were filled with Alka-Seltzer carried us out of the forest and into the parking lot of a local strip mall.

As our little combat boots went from mud to concrete we looked up and saw the large gray speaker that stood atop of the telephone pole wailing as it slowly turned and howled out its siren call. But cars were driving, people were walking, and the local Chicken Hut still had its "Open for Business" sign hanging in their window.

We made a dash to the open garage of a heavy utilities rental company. Inside were two older men working on a lawnmower. Grabbing our knees, coughing, and gasping for air, Kevin blurted out, "Are we at war?!?"

The two men looked confused. The one with a silver wrench in his hand said, "Excuse me, son?"

"IS THIS A NUCLEAR WAR!?!?!?!"

The man looked at his friend and began to smile, "No, son." The smile broke into a condescending chuckle, "Those are the new tornado sirens. They test 'em every Tuesday at 10:30 AM."

We were stunned. I turned and looked at my friends. Most of them were still panting from sprinting uphill through the trees and bushes, everyone's cheeks and foreheads had little red cuts from tree branches hitting their faces. A few were still sobbing, the remnants of the adrenaline still working its way through their veins, and I stood sopping wet with mud covering half of my camouflaged body. I looked at Jerry and he looked at me, and together we let out what might be the biggest sigh of relief either of us had known in our entire lives. Smiling, Jerry looked at me and said, "Man, you screamed like a little girl."

A nervous laughter arose from the small mob. Straightening up and with a serious face I said, "Pssh, you were scared because you thought it was a nuclear war too." His eyes squinted like he wanted to fight me for calling him out.

That day, in that garage, our gang of misfits stood luminous and brilliant. Despite the muffled sobs, the tears, and the mud, it was a perfect moment. One simple yet magic day in a host of thousands when time was infinite and golden. Here, nothing mattered outside of friends, mayhem, and microwaveable pizza rolls. Right then, in that garage, despite the mud dripping from my camouflaged body, I felt the magic in the air. It was the first time I felt true companionship. I stood amongst heroes. In my world, at that very second no one understood me more than they did. It was an awakening, and in that instant I felt lucky, lucky that I was in their presence, and while I may have not had the ability to convey my love for them, I looked back at Jerry, waited a beat, and cracked a smile.

"Come on man," I put my arm on his shoulder and said, "Let's all go back to my house and watch 'Commando'."

Fireworks are for Suckers

ഇൗരു

She somehow got rooftop seating at a Cubs game. I hated sports and so did she but we knew it was a way to be together, away from the eyes of our friends and the one who didn't want us to be together. We sat and ignored the game until it was dark. Behind us there were fireworks. I held her hand and I kissed her. She knew I shouldn't. I knew she shouldn't. I didn't care. So we did. We were both single but we couldn't be together. Ever. We kissed on a perfect summer evening on the top of a building sitting on bleachers while fireworks were exploding. It was stupid and cliché and typical and magic and magic and magic. I loved her so hard my chest trembled.

We are Unbreakable

ঠ০জ

Clothes are raining down on me.

The sun is just breaking through the early morning clouds and I'm smashed between forty thousand anxious people, and I'm freezing.

It's 44 degrees this morning and I'm wearing tiny blue shorts with no underwear and a black band T-shirt that I have every intention of throwing away in about ten minutes.

I am enveloped by young and old and black and white and brown and thick and skinny. We are one mass. Corralled so closely I cannot even make out the pavement below. If I lifted my feet I would remain upright. We are one mass, alive and buzzing with nervous energy.

And clothes are raining down on me.

I look to my right, left, front, back and see nothing but a sea of people. Everyone is touching me. The man behind me is holding my shoulder to balance while he stands on one foot and ties his shoe. He didn't ask. Nor did the middle-aged women in yellow whose back and ass continue to rub up against my leg and arm. I can only see people, and above, gray sky.

The sky is alive with clothes. Thousands of windbreakers and track pants shooting up and arcing back into the sea. Red, yellow, blue, orange, purple flying through the air. Discarded. Raining down on everyone.

We are all waiting. Waiting for the sound of the air horn.

I listen.

"Oh, say can you see..."

The national anthem.

I take a deep breath and hold it in and I think about how I am only minutes away from testing every cell and fiber in my body. My eyes roll back and I point my nose to the sky. I can only hear my heart thumping wildly. I exhale and it slows. I take another deep breath and unclench my fists. My nerves and the cold cause my legs to begin jumping in place.

This is it. This is what it all comes down to.

Stay calm. Breathe. Slow.

"For the land of the free..."

Eyes closed. Breathe deep.

"And the home..."

Relax. This is it.

"Of the..."

Hold the breath. Breathing paused. My eyes are squeezed tight. I can feel tingles in the tips of my fingers.

"Braaaaave."

Applause.

The air horn sounds and forty thousand people begin running in place. I stand still. I know well enough to take every opportunity to conserve my energy. I stand still and I breathe and I wait.

Several minutes later we begin to move slowly. First walking, then fast walking, and as I pass over the START line I begin running at a brisk pace. The mass thins out slightly and I notice thousands of people standing on each side of the street clapping and waving at no one and everyone in particular. I smile and think about how simple the gesture is. All around me are thousands of people, running in front, behind, to the sides, zigzagging for a better position. Slowing down, speeding up, catching up to friends, waving to spectators. I maintain my pace and put my headphones on.

I am doing this without their help.

This is it. This is what I've trained for, summer after summer.

This is what the sun and the rain and the Chicago winters of snow and ice and hail tried to beat out of me. This is the first and only thing in my life that I have attempted with absolutely no help from anyone. This is my heart put to the test. The question looms in the back of my mind: What will give out first, Chris? Your body, or your will?

This is it. Mile one.

The atmosphere is chaotic and festive. Smiles and laughs between friends, silly hats and spectators waving homemade banners and signs of support all give the illusion that this is a celebration.

I know better.

I know because I've heard the accounts of bruises, cuts, breaks, sprains, dehydration, vomiting, defecation, heat stroke, heart attack, and death.

Clap and smile all you want.

I press play and the music reduces the crowd to a dull roar. Watching the pavement to avoid more discarded clothes I think about how good my body feels right now. Awake and wide eyed, teeming with sugars and carbohydrates from a week's worth of pasta dinners, I want to sprint, to break away from the slower runners but I must conserve. My legs feel strong and confident, my lungs are using so little energy that I calmly breathe through my nose. My form is rigid yet fluid, I am a machine built for one purpose. To maintain.

Perfect.

I settle in, maintain my pace, and leap from time to time to avoid piles of discarded clothing, and I smile. I smile because in a few hours, I know I won't.

We take our first turn and head downtown, swallowed by the shadows of the skyscrapers. The white noise created by the sounds of thousands seeps its way into my ears. I turn up the volume on my headphones. I don't want any of their support. I need to know my body and my will and my heart can do this on their own.

My body is warm from the cotton shirt, but cotton is a long distance runner's worst enemy. The constant wet rubbing turns the innocent shirt into a giant piece of fine grit sandpaper that will, with time, wear away at your skin on your shoulders, armpits and nipples. I pull my shirt over my head and throw it back into the sea of people behind me. It is now only my shoes and my shorts and my headphones and my will.

Miles 2, 3 and 4 wind through the canyons of concrete, iron, and glass. Past courthouses and financial institutions, past towering monuments to consumerism and commerce. Each mile marker displays a time. I am doing well. The strides I make are deliberate and precisely measured. I have found my groove. Mile after mile my body feels stronger.

Mile five pushes us out of the belly of the downtown concrete canyons and into the nearby yuppie neighborhoods. Children lean out the windows of million dollar brownstone homes built by turn of the century wealthy industrialists, and they bang on pots. Yuppies nursing hangovers with grande lattes toast us as we speed past their front porches. Mothers and fathers and sons and daughters hold up florescent pink signs that read cheesy motivational clichés.

I appreciate their effort and support.

But I smile an evil grin because I know I don't need it.

Each approaching mile brings a hydration station. Long tables set up along the sides of the street with thousands of cups of water and Gatorade handed out by teenage girls who were most likely conned into volunteering by their high school track coach.

I weave my way to the side, stick out my hand and grab a cup from the girls.

"Thank you so much," I say, because no one else does.

Immediately I am splashed with water. I look to my right and see runners grabbing two and three cups at a time, most of which are dropped or spilled on nearby runners. I am tightly packed in and my already cold legs get drenched, as does everyone else around me. Thousands of discarded cups litter the streets like a welcome home parade sponsored by Hinckley and Schmidt has just passed. I make my way back into the middle of the mass, burp, and continue to ignore everyone around me.

I focus on the songs. I focus on the shirt of the woman in front of me. It reads, "This is for my mom."

I get spit on.

"Sorry," a man says.

I shrug.

Minutes later, I get spit on by a woman. There is no apology.

This happens every few minutes.

I am a machine.

Steady and perfect pace. Chin up. Chest forward. Arms flexed at no more than a 90-degree angle. I find the lines on the road and I follow them. Heel, toe. Heel, toe. Relaxed breathing. This is easy.

At mile 6 I recall the years I have spent leading up to this moment. From the first moment I strapped on shoes to run around my block, to each and every lung steaming, leg cramping, shin splinting run along lake Michigan, this is what it was all for.

This very second. This very step.

Hundreds of Gatorades.

Multiple sprained ankles.

Countless worn and abandoned shoes.

Each watery-eyed training run was about this second.

This step.

I will not fail. If I have to die doing this, so be it.

So be it if I break or sprain something.

So be it if my lungs burn and my heart breaks.

I will not fail.

If I have an ounce of fight left in me at mile 26, I will use it. If I have to crawl and claw my way to that finish line, then

God damn everything, I will do it. I smile because my body feels good and I smile because I know that my will has just burned its bridges with my body and told it to fuck off. I nod my head and I smile.

Mile 7 we enter Boystown, a gay and wonderful neighborhood. The drag queens come out in elaborate costumes and cheer us on. I recognize a few spectators. They don't notice me.

Miles 8, 9, 10, 11 and 12 are nothing.

I have a light sheen of sweat on my body and I feel as if I could run forever. I breath shallow and through my nose. This is easy. I am a machine.

Mile 13 is the halfway point somewhere in the neighborhood of the West Loop. There is great fanfare and balloons and loud mouthed radio station DJs singing along with Bon Jovi. I take out my left headphone to listen.

"Wooooah, we're HALFWAY THERE..."

Are you fucking kidding me?

"WOOOOOAHH, we're LIVIN' ON A PRAYER!"

Typical and obvious.

I scoff, shake my head, spit on the ground and put my headphone back in my ear and begin singing my own anthems written by dirt poets sung with gutter mouths.

I'm halfway and I'm still singing. I'm still smiling my evil grin. I'm still able to take in and appreciate the beauty of the old buildings in the amazing neighborhoods of this wonderful city. I'm still breathing through my nose. I retain my perfect form and I think I may actually be able to do this.

Miles 14 and 15 are the same.

Mile 16 is where I feel my body begin to slouch.

I am in complete control but I feel my resources depleting quickly. At the hydration station I stick my hand out and grab two Gatorades and a Powergel shot.

A Powergel shot is a concentrated goo consisting of caffeine and sugary simple carbohydrates with the consistency of warm mayonnaise. I tear open the foil top and squeeze the contents into my mouth and throw the wrapper on the ground. I swallow and my body lurches forward. Maybe I have overestimated myself. This shot throws a monkey wrench in the machine. I hiccup and the sugary mayonnaise makes an attempt at coming back up my throat. I gather the last of the saliva that remains in my mouth and my tongue forcefully shoves the contents back down into my stomach.

I open my mouth and begin breathing through it. I try to steady myself. Breathe. You are fine. Breathe. Keep moving. Don't stop.

My legs are tired. My lungs seemed to have shrunk a bit. My chin is heavy. My shoulders want to let my arms drop.

Ten miles. That's all. Ten more miles.

Mile 17 never comes. I've been running for what seems like an hour and I haven't seen mile 17. I know I'm on course but a slight yet unreasonable panic sets in, reminiscent of being lost in the supermarket when you were a child.

I take my headphones out and I speak for the first time.

"Excuse me," I say to a dark haired man running next to me.

"Yes?"

"Um, have you seen mile 17?" I ask in a shaky childlike voice.

"Well, there's mile 18," he says, pointing to the upcoming mile marker.

A calm rushes over me. I missed it.

But how could I have missed it? Each mile marker has tremendous signs flashing the time and hundreds of girls handing out water and Gatorade. How could I miss this? My eyes grow and wildly scan the area for an indication of my progress; a shiver runs down to my guts. I zoned out so much I missed the past two miles.

This scares me. I have never not been in complete in control of my body and I don't like it. My mind is slipping.

I shake my hands, I shake my head back and forth and I begin slapping my face. It burns and I don't know why. Focus. Focus on the crowd and the signs and the people around you. Stimulation, your body needs stimulation. I look around, I take deep breaths and I take in the sights and the colors and the smells.

This is a bad idea.

Why are there ambulances everywhere? Why are people on stretchers? Why do all these people have oxygen masks on? Why are people running with what looks to be diarrhea trickling down their legs?

"UUUMMMFF." I hear what sounds like someone slapping the side of beef. I look to my right and see a woman on the asphalt who had just fallen on her chest and her face. Her arms still at her sides, she didn't have time to brace her fall. For a second I see her face look my way and her eyes closed in pain. I see blood coming from her right cheek. Then I see the mass overtake her. No one stops. They run, stumble and fall over her. It is a horrifying sight. A few runners eventually stop and try to help her up but they are overtaken as well.

This is serious.

There are no more smiling faces.

I slap my chest and my face and my neck and say aloud, "Wake up, wake up." Maintain. Maintain, Chris. Keep moving forward and in less than an hour this will all be over. You got this motherfucker. This road will not take your spirit. You are stronger than these fuckers. They couldn't live your life. They don't have the balls to live on brains and guts and mayhem like you do. They are automatons, they are sheep and lemmings and robots. They have no heart. None of these fuckers have the heart you have today. None.

"HOLY FUCK!" I scream.

I look down to see what I stepped on and there is nothing there.

I step again.

"YEEEOOOW!"

Each step on my right foot delivers a red-hot, sharp pain in the arch of my foot.

Every other step feels like a thick spike is drilling deeper and deeper into my foot.

I have to stop. I can't take it.

The machine yells back at me, "Are you dead yet?"

My will says "No."

The machine says, "Then keep moving forward."

And I do. I hobble but I move forward maintaining my pace. Clearly favoring my right foot.

Mile 19. The pain subsides but does not completely disappear. The consequence of favoring my right foot is a new pain in my left knee that I must endure to compensate for the weight from my right foot.

Mile 20.

Mile 21. Chinatown. People in large dragon costumes line the streets and the spectators are alive and buzzing. I recognize some faces and they recognize me.

A sign reads: YOUR ONLY LIMITATIONS ARE SELF-IMPOSED.

I note my posture and I square my shoulders and I raise my chin because I refuse to show weakness. Maintain. Maintain through the pain. Just as quickly as we entered Chinatown we are leaving it. Up and over century-old iron bridges and into the ghetto. There is only a sparse crowd of spectators, mostly Mexican. I see vendors selling horchata and coconut ice cream like my father used to buy me when I was young. Two young girls have set up a small yellow table and are handing out Dixie cups of lemonade. None of the runners are taking the cups from the girls and I see how the girls' eyes grow wide, then how their faces fall as everyone ignores them.

I begin shoving my way though the yuppies with heart monitors and $400 pace counting watches and $300 custom built running shoes, and I make my way towards the two little brown girls.

A blonde woman shoves me back and I don't care.

I make it to their table just in time and I hold out my hand. They both get excited and each hand me a cup. Not breaking stride I lean down and I smile and I say "Thank you so much." And I pat the one with pigtails on the head. I see her turn to her friend, smile, and put her hands to her face.

I smile and my eyes water because of their innocence. I turn and face forward and my eyes water because I hate each and every one of these arrogant motherfuckers around me. I hate them for passing right by the two little girls in the ghetto. A rage builds and my body gets stronger. Careful not to spill any, I drink the last of my lemonade and I run. I run for every little kid that got passed over by people without time. I run for the disapproving looks from the runners who scoff at my shitty clothes, my shitty tattoos, and my shitty running shoes, and who say with their face, "What the fuck is HE doing here?" But most of all I run because I won't let this road beat me.

I see the mile marker for mile 22 and what was once difficult has now become grueling and agonizing.

I make my way to the tables on the sides, pushing my way through runners with closed eyes, and I extend my arms and grab whatever is available. My strides are no longer perfect and precise. They are clomping along, independent of my body they are merely an extension of my knees that somehow manage to keep moving forward.

I am no longer in control of my lower body. I do not physically control my hips. They move because they have been for 4 hours and no one has told them to stop. My back has lurched forward, my shoulders slope, and my arms, once flexed at 90 degree angles in front on me are now at 20 degree angles dangling at my sides.

Thirty more minutes. You are not dead yet.

Mile marker 23. I see the hydration tables and I make my way to them. It's easier this time because the mass has thinned to a trickle of zombies. Some crying, some angry, some asleep yet moving forward. I stick out my arm and I grab a much-needed Gatorade. I put it to my nose and my lips and it smells like urine. I look and see a shirtless drunk asshole in his mid-twenties holding a bottle of beer and he's yelling. I take out my right earphone.

"FREE BEER!" he yells with a smile.

My lips tense and I clench my jaw and I throw the cup of beer back at him and yell, "You fucking asshole!"

He looks at me confused.

I'm losing it.

Mile marker 24.

Ok Chris, two more miles and it will all be over. It will be over and no one will ever be able to take this away from you. I feel my eyes begin to close. The machine is shutting down rapidly.

I slap my face and it burns and I don't know why.

I want to sleep.

Sleep in my soft bed.

I want to drink a lake of water.

I want to stop moving. I just want to stop moving.

I want to sleep.

I feel woozy. I begin to stumble to the left. I feel this coming, my mind is aware of my body but my body isn't responding.

Wake up. Wake up.

"YEEEEOOOOW!" I scream.

The pain in my right foot shoots up through my leg, into my chest and straight to my right temple.

I am awake but in excruciating pain.

"HOLY FUUUUUUUUUCK!" I yell.

Every other step blinds me. My right temple throbs one second after my foot touches the ground.

Two more miles. Fuck. Fuck. Fuck.

"Ok Chris, you're not dead yet are you?" The machine asks.

"FUCK NO!" I yell.

"Are you a fucking pussy?" The machine asks.

I don't answer.

"ARE YOU A FUCKING PUSSY?"

"FUCK NO!"

I pick my head up, I crush my teeth together, and I tell my heart this will be over in a matter of minutes.

My lungs are filled with acid.

I slap my face and it burns. I look down at my hands and they are covered in salt crystals from the evaporating sweat. I wipe my brow with the back of my hand and my hand is white with salt. The salt begins to run into my eyes. My face, my neck and my eyes are now on fire. A part of me is happy that I don't have to concentrate solely on the white-hot piercing pain in my temple or the dull and deep pain in my left knee.

I cannot see. My eyes are filled with stinging water and I cannot see. My lungs are battery acid. I can't breath deep enough. I can't get enough air.

I look down at my shoes soaked in Gatorade, water, sweat and spit and I see red spots on the tops of my shoes. My toes are bleeding.

"You're going to be ok, Chris. You will live," the machine says.

"Fifteen more minutes and no one can ever take this from you," the machine says.

"You're not dead yet," the machine says.

"You can still put one foot in front of the other."

I try to smile but my face can't manage to do anything but wince from the pain.

I see mile marker 25 and a woman running next to me unknowingly spits on my face. I don't care.

A man spits on me.

I keep moving.

A man falls from exhaustion. No one stops to help.

There are medics all around affixing oxygen masks on fallen and defeated men and women, young and old, black and white.

My form is that of an old woman stumbling down a steep hill. If a small gust of wind hit me it could knock me to the ground. I want to stop. My body wants to stop. I just want to stop.

My mouth is white and dry.

My lips are cracked and salty.

My eyes burn deep in their sockets.

My legs move as two autonomous hunks of meat, merely flailing my calves and feet forward.

The air is so thin I breathe like a rabbit on speed.

Each step is pain like I've never felt.

Each step is exhaustion attacking my will.

"Almost there, Chris," I tell myself.

"Almost there."

Ahead I see the slight incline of a hill and I curse god himself. There is no way I can make this. No way.

I look around me and notice I am alone. The runners who have surrounded me for twenty-five and a half miles are now keeping their distance. They are looking at me and I don't know why.

I take off my headphones and I hear someone screaming like a raving lunatic.

Someone is screaming obscenities like they're being murdered. Shrill and high-pitched, I hear it in my ears. I look to the left and everyone is glaring at me, I look to the right and they are keeping their distance.

I lost it.

It's me.

The pep talks I thought I was having with myself in my head were actually screaming, foaming-at-the-mouth, out-loud tirades that scared the others away. I listen to myself.

"YOU FUCKING PUSSY!"

"YOU FUCKING PUSSY!"

"YOU. ARE. NOT. FUCKING. DEAD. YET. YOU. FUCKING. SON. OF. A. BITCH."

"FUCK!"

"FUCK!"

The words are loud, they are coming from my mouth and I don't know who is saying them. My eyes scan around in confusion and my head can't make my mouth stop.

I am truly no longer in control of my facilities.

The machine has stormed the castle and is now running the show.

"YOU HAVE NO FUCKING HEART."

"YOU'RE NOT DEAD YET! YOU KEEP FUCKING MOVING!"

I look down. My feet still move. One. Two. One. Two.

I am detached.

Completely detached.

My eyes watch in horror as my body has been taken over by a masochistic demon with a foul mouth.

I look to the spectators lining the streets. The crowd here is thick because they came to see the victories. They are screaming and cheering and smiling. I watch as the happiness melts away from their faces when they see the spit-covered, hobbling, salt-encrusted, obscenity demon coming their way. My eyes say I'm sorry. But the machine has complete domination.

I turn the corner am I see it. It's in the distance but it clearly reads, FINISH. I am about 300 feet away and I don't know if I can make it.

"FUCK YOU!" my mouth yells at the sign.

The machine knows that that sign is the cause and the breakdown. The machine knows that that sign is the cause of the greatest physical pain and exhaustion and thirst it has ever known.

"FUCK YOU, YOU SON OF BITCH!"

Clop. Clop. Clop. I look at my feet. The spots of blood on the tops of my shoes are growing larger but somehow my feet still function.

I am seconds away from the sign. I am surrounded by thousands of people staring at me. Thousands.

The machine is yelling.

Screaming like a madman.

I cross the finish line and my slabs of meat do not stop. They keep me moving. They don't know how to stop. I take my weary arms and push down on my knees and they still keep moving.

I yell, "STOP!" And after an additional 10 steps they come to a reluctant halt.

I find myself standing in a line. There is a group of people are handing out thin foil blankets to help us keep the warmth in. I rest my hands on my knees and I say quietly to myself, "You did it, son. They couldn't break you."

The demon is gone.

I smile.

And I begin to laugh.

Tears form because this is what I've dreamt about for years and I laugh uncontrollably.

I laugh because I know I beat the odds.

I laugh because I know I beat their stares and condescension.

I laugh because this moment is surreal.

But truly I laugh because if I don't I will break down and die.

I look to the sky, now blue, and the sun shines for me.

I am unbreakable.

Unbreakable.

Heart-Games and Head-Cases

છુૂૃ૩

We had one date. One date and I was infatuated. I was a grown man and I was acting like a little kid checking my phone for missed calls. She was playing the game. The game I knew. The game I played. And I was falling for it. And I knew it. But I fell for it. I couldn't help it. She finally called a week later and told me she was sick. I told her I wanted to see her. She said she wasn't getting out of bed. I told her I didn't care. She said "Ok." I raced to the store and bought supplies then I raced at 90 mph to get to her apartment in the city. 26 minutes. Unheard of. I parked almost a mile away in the snow. I took my skateboard out of the back seat and rested the groceries on the nose while carrying two other full paper bags. I pushed and pushed along the wet streets sweating profusely. I wanted to see her smell her touch her be next to her more than anything. Ever. I got in the elevator, pushed 17 and rode it up to the top. She opened the door and she had orange hair. I laughed and she coughed. She asked what was in all the bags. I told her chicken noodle soup, ginger ale, crackers, vitamin C, cookies, Gatorade and orange juice: two types, one with and one without pulp. I read Hemingway to her until she fell asleep that night.

She Was Way Too Cool for Me

ഇരു

She was a metal version of Madonna.

Platinum blonde hair, big boobs and a love for Motley Crüe. She taunted me from the front of Mr. Bernal's English literature class.

I didn't have to speak to her. I couldn't, even if I wanted to. I was young and new to taking risks and she was confident and intimidating and beautiful. I spent the semester trying to devise a plan to speak to her. I figured, maybe I could ask her for a pen, or I could ask her when the date of the next test would be. But as circumstance would have it, whenever our desks were repositioned I somehow found myself on the opposite end of the room, admiring the black bra that showed through her white T-shirt from afar.

I imagined kissing her. I thought about what it would feel like to have my lips touch hers. To be so intimate that our faces were touching and yet not feeling totally grossed out. I practiced it on the back of my hand.

I watched the movies intensely.

Slowly, not too aggressive. A little tongue, not too much. Closed eyes and relaxed. I wanted to kiss her.

The last day of school came to an end with the sound of the early release bell. For a town littered with latch key kids from single parent homes, this meant one thing: a half-day of unsupervised mayhem.

The band of punk skater kids I hung out with were known more for peeing on things than for picking up chicks, but that day we had managed to coerce a handful of cute girls to hang out with us. We walked to a random girl's house whose parents weren't around and immediately found all that was flammable and began sacrificing her belongings to the god of arson. Set to the soundtrack of the Sex Pistols, the smell of smoke permeated the air while we ransacked the house like a group of adolescent Vikings, stealing and pillaging everything in sight. That is, until the door opened and SHE walked in wearing a tight blue T-shirt.

I froze at the top of the stairs when she looked up at me. I felt my eyes grow as large as saucers. I felt like I had been punched in the gut. Run. Run. Run or she will notice you staring.

And that's exactly what I did. I ran into the next room.

"Stephanie is here," I yelled, playing it cool as if my heart wasn't already in my throat.

She walked up the stairs, surveyed the anarchy and without missing a beat or batting an eye she said, "Hey."

That's it. "Hey." She was so cool.

She asked me for my lighter so she could show me a trick. My dry mouth barely managed to squeeze out the word, "Sure."

Our hands touched. I felt the warmth of her white skin and she became real. I thought, if I could touch her, then that was one step closer to her becoming my girlfriend. She was the first girl to set me off. To make my heart race and to make me want to write corny I-love-you poetry like in the movies. She was my 8th grade perfection.

"Give me that bottle of mousse from that table over there," she commanded.

"Why?"

"Just do it."

I leaned back and grabbed the black canister of mousse and handed it to her. She took it and sprayed a large mass of expanding hair product into her hand.

Then she demanded, "Now hand me the lighter."

I handed her the lighter and with one flick of her finger she ignited the white foam.

WHOOSH.

The mousse went up in a bright orange fireball.

She was so cool.

She was so cool I couldn't breathe. That was until I heard the jingle of keys.

"Shit, my mom's home. Get the fuck out," the random girl screamed.

We grabbed our skateboards, stole whatever trinkets of value off the shelves that we could, yelled goodbye and made a mad dash out the sliding glass backdoor.

Reeking of smoke, we set our skateboards down, counted up our bounty, considered it a success and parted ways.

I skated two miles home with a smile on my face. I had my first serious crush.

That night during dinner the phone rang.

"Hey, Chris?" the girl said.

"Yes?"

"Stephanie likes you. You should call her."

This moment would go down in history as the first time I had ever played it cool.

"Really? She's cute. Give me her number."

I returned to the kitchen table smiling ear-to-ear and clearly unable to finish my dinner.

My mom looked up from her plate and said "go call her" with a wink of an eye.

I looked up at her from my cold green beans, smiled, shoved myself away from the table and rushed up the stairs taking three at a time.

"Um, hi...is Stephanie there?" I asked.

"This is."

Six hours later I said, "So, um...will you go out with me?"

"Yes."

I hung up the phone at 3 a.m., closed my eyes, raised my head and let out a sigh. She was my girlfriend. This was it, the first time I was giving my heart away. My heart notified my face and we all felt warm, fuzzy and tingly all over. I never needed to see or hear from another person again. It was just us.

It was now officially summer, which meant that us boys tried to wear as little clothing as possible, cause as much trouble as we could get away with and skate as much as our little legs would carry us...or at least until the streetlights came on. Every day we would stop by Stephanie's house to raid her refrigerator and throw each other into her swimming pool. And every day I would leave her with a hug.

See, I never wanted to leave when we were at Stephanie's because leaving meant having to say goodbye. And saying goodbye meant having to hug her. And having to hug her meant I might have to KISS her. And god knows that this timid and inexperienced hundred pound weakling wasn't ready for that.

Two weeks into our whirlwind summer romance my friend Tim looks over at me and says, "Dude, did you make out with Stephanie yet?"

"No, I...," I pause and hold my breath. "I've never kissed a girl."

Tim looks at me with his mouth open wide in disbelief.

"ARE YOU FUCKING KIDDING ME? YOU HAVENT KISSED HER?"

"Dude, don't tell anyone. I don't want everyone to know I'm lame," I say with a quivering bottom lip.

"Nah dude, I won't tell anyone." Tim says with an evil grin.

My admission did nothing but set into motion a chain of events the next day that would lead to the most scarring and emotionally torturous moment of my life.

The next day came and we casually skated up to Stephanie's driveway to feast upon her newly stocked freezer of microwavable dinners. My friend John rings her doorbell, looks over his shoulder and says, "So, I hear you haven't kissed her yet."

I glare daggers at him.

Tim smiles back with the fuck-you face.

Turning around and facing me, John says, "Oh, you're going to make out with her today."

Running away at this point would be instant social suicide. I smiled back like I was too cool for school and said "whatever." Had I not just peed on the bush down the block, urine surely would have been dripping from my shorts that very moment.

I look through the screen door and see Stephanie jump down her stairs onto the landing. She's bouncy and energetic today. "What's up?"

"What is up is that I heard you guys haven't made out yet," John says.

My face goes hot and I want to fight each and every one of my friends.

She laughs and says, "Oh, who gives a shit."

She was cool.

Too cool to notice my pulsating bright red ears.

We walk in and begin pillaging. I throw a box of frozen French fries into the microwave, jump up on the kitchen counter and take my position next to Stephanie. My friends turn to me.

"So, you guys should go make out now," John says, staring directly at me.

I go white and they laugh out loud.

"Chris doesn't have..."

Stephanie is cut short by the mob that has now grabbed each of us by the arms and is shoving us towards the bathroom.

This isn't happening. I panic.

They jump on my back and take me down to the ground. Tim stands and grabs my legs and begins dragging me closer and closer to the bathroom. I'm panicking. I'm clawing at the carpet with my fingers and it burns. I'm grabbing at wood paneling. I feel hot. I feel dizzy. I want to scream. My jaw is clenched tight. My eyes are frantically scanning back and forth looking for something, anything to hang on to. But it's too late. My fingers begin clawing at tile and I know. I know I'm in the bathroom. I look up and the door slams shut.

Stephanie is standing in the bathroom smiling.

She finds this funny.

She's not nervous. She's made out with boys before. High school boys. How can I possibly compete with high school boys?

"And we're not letting you out until she says you guys have made out!" John yells through the door.

Instantly my foot begins tapping furiously. I look at the floor and I start scratching the back of my neck. My heart is racing.

"Are you nervous?" she asks.

"Um yeah, a little," I say as I'm dying. The air is thin in the bathroom. I can't breathe.

"It's cool. Just relax," she says, doing her best to comfort me.

At this point my legs won't stop shaking. I notice because today I decided to wear my tight gray skate shorts, and nothing else. My body trembles like a deep, chest-piercing cold has set in. My teeth begin to chatter. I close my mouth tight.

Stephanie's eyes fall and she says, "Just come here and hug me. It's no big deal." She wraps her arms around me.

I know she can feel my heart beat on her chest. The thumping is so loud I can hear it inside my ears. I don't hug her back. I keep my hands close to my chest. She continues to hug me.

"You don't have to do this if you don't want to."

But I do. I want her to know I do. She's every bit of every girl I've ever wanted. I love her. I want nothing more in this world than to kiss her, but that's why this is so difficult. I wish I could tell her this but I can't get the words to form on my tongue.

Instead I tremble.

"Ok, look at me."

I pull away and look at her. She's smiling. It's comfortable. She's staring right into me and she's smiling. She's so beautiful. Her eyes, her hair, her skin, her breasts, her uncanny ability to tell me she loves me at the exact moment I need to hear it. I want to kiss her but my compulsion to run has a much better grip on my legs. I turn away.

"Stop," she snaps. "Look at me."

I take a deep breath and I look at her. I stare at her for a moment and let it out. Her eyes begin to close and her face becomes more relaxed.

Her eyes become slits.

This is it.

She puts her hands on my shoulders.

This is it.

She begins pulling me in.

My heart is going to explode. It's beating so hard it hurts.

Her lips are now inches away from my lips.

No. No. No.

I smell her breath and I turn away.

Quickly I snap my head to the side and I hug her. I hold her tight. As tight as I can. I can't do this. I can't. I wont look her in the eyes again. I should leave. I wasn't built for this. My little heart cant take this anymore. Make this end. Please god, make it end. Don't make me have to kiss her.

She sighs. She's disappointed. Tolerant, but disappointed.

"You don't have to do this if you don't want to." I can hear her fuse getting shorter.

"I know," I say. "I'm just, I'm just nervous around you."

I feel small. I feel like a sad a pathetic little boy. I'm half naked, shaking, with a white streak of fear down my spine. The air is heavy and electric.

"Ok. One more time. Are you ready?" she says.

"Yes."

"Ok."

This time she gets a solid grip on my shoulders and squares them in alignment with hers. She does this to ensure I won't run. She slowly pulls my body closer to hers.

I step toward her and feel the bathmat beneath my feet. I see her skin getting closer. Her lips. The air is heavy. Closer. I smell her breath. My hands are shivering on her shoulders. I'm too scared to care. She's inches away. Her eyes close. My eyes close. And we meet.

The touch is warm and wet. She opens her mouth and I open mine because that's what they do in the movies. I feel her tongue on my tongue and my body goes stiff. Oh god. I can't breathe. I can't breathe.

The feeling is similar to when you can't breathe in that mid-vomit sort of panic way. I can't breathe. She's sucking the oxygen out of me. Her tongue is moving around with mine. Oh god. Make it stop. Make it stop. The fear washes from the back of my head down my spine like a cold bucket of water and I can't move. I want to push away but the electricity connects us. I can't move. I can't breathe. God, why can't I push away.

Push, goddamn it.

PUSH.

I begin to push on her shoulders with all the might I have but my strength is being sucked out of me.

Push, damn you. PUSH.

My body is stiff and rigid and I push. With all I have left in me I turn my head and shove her away.

I gasp for air as if I've been underwater for five minutes. My arms are still stiff, slightly bent in front of me like a zombie. My eyes couldn't be wider. My mouth hangs slightly open and I'm looking around like I've just been scared awake.

Holy shit that couldn't have gone worse.

Oh.

But it could.

I look down and I notice I've got the biggest, meanest, most intense solid fucking oak hard-on peeking its way out of the top of my tight ass shorts.

AAAAHHH!

I scream and I rush toward the door, knocking Stephanie out of the way, ripping the door open and bowling over my four friends standing guard.

"Whoa dude, where are you running to?" John laughs.

I sprint down the hallway to Stephanie's room with the strongest erection I have ever had banging up against my stomach. I rush into her room, jump on to her bed, lie on my stomach and pull the covers over me.

Think of dead kittens. Think of dead kittens.

Goddamn it, this thing isn't going away.

Dead kittens. Dead kittens.

I look up and see my friends walk into the room laughing.

Please don't tell me they saw it. Please.

"Dude, congratulations. You just had your first make out," John says as they all start patting me on the back.

I look up and see Stephanie walk into the room.

"Yeah, it was cool," I say with a bit of swag and I look up at her.

She just looks back at me and smiles. Because even at the age of 13 she knew how to keep a secret.

She was cool.

Way too cool for me.

The Princess of Diversey Avenue

ഗ‌ാര

We laughed as we walked east on Diversey Avenue and I tripped her from behind because I was more of an annoying little brother than a boyfriend. My princess stood to my right while I held the white plastic bags of take-out Mexican food. The sun was in what movie directors refer to as "the magic hour," when the world is basked in an orangey glow and is reminiscent of late night summertime little league games and fourth of July picnics. The air smelled of youth and innocence.

We walked and we laughed and we held the ends of each other's pinky fingers the way teenagers do when they walk in the mall. Approaching us was a dark, sloping figure completely covered in oversized, dirty rags. Its head was down and it was aggressively marching forward. "Fuck you, you nigger bitch!" The figure screamed.

My feet stopped and my stomach dropped. The figure moved behind us.

"Get your finger out of my ass you fucking nigger bitch!" The figure yelled while raising a fist. The fist was cocking back, its angle of trajectory was not aimed at me but at the girl that I kissed goodnight. I threw my body in-between the two, pulled my elbow as far back as I could stretch, closed my fingers tight and with the force to punch a hole through bone, my fist raged forward into the dirty face of rage and rags.

"Uuh!" The figure yelled as it fell to the ground.

I lunged forward with teeth bared, steel in my eyes and bricks for fists.

"Don't you fucking hit me!" The creature screamed. I could see now that the heap of dirt and rags was a middle-aged, homeless woman lying on her back. She propped herself up on her elbows and said, "She's the one who put her finger in my ass!"

I stood above the woman with a fury that could only be described as a combination of the last five seconds of dirty sex and the terror of a haunted house. I wanted to smash her face in for even entertaining the idea of touching the girl who owned my heart. I wanted to tear the filthy gray brown matted hair from her head, I wanted to spit obscenities in her face, and my knuckles craved nothing more than to crash into her eye-sockets...but she was probably someone's mother. A woman. A woman who was forced to endure this world with her brain misfiring so much so that she was unaware, or was left without the capacity to care that bugs lived on her skin. And all that came through my teeth was, "You motherfucker." I picked up the white plastic bags, shook my head, and we continued to walk down Diversey Avenue.

The Last of the Great Misanthropes

✂꧁꧂

As the side door of the van slid open, the cold sting of a Canadian January wind smacked my right cheek with the intensity of a recoiling rubber band.

"Ah fuck," I yelped, squinting my eyes and holding my right hand up to protect my face from the midnight air. "You sure this is the right place?"

"Yeah. This is the only Burger King around here."

A week prior, the band I played bass guitar in embarked on what would be one of the single most intelligent ideas we had collectively agreed upon: to tour the northeast United States and Canada in the dead of winter. It being in the negative digits didn't help much, nor did the blizzard that caused near white-out conditions in the vast expanses of eastern Canada. But were stubborn than determined and no one ever wants to be the guy who chimes in, "But it's COLD outside." But the weather was just the beginning of our problems.

Nine boys, comprising two lackluster bands, piled in to a white cargo van on a chilly Chicago morning to begin our whirlwind two-week tour. We were going to take over the world by sharing guitars and amplifiers with opening bands, and play our hearts and throats out to anyone who would listen. That year we had managed to save enough money from playing dingy bowling alleys and basement shows to purchase a van. The van was a not so gently used former flower delivery van. This van was all business...meaning it wasn't built with luxuries like air conditioning, am/fm radio, or carpet. If it was legally possible to get away with foregoing front seats, I'm sure the previous owners would have torn those out as well. All this luxury for a mere $1000. The only remaining characteristics from its commercial days were two red flower decals that clung to each side, which we left on as a reminder of its previous life.

The interior looked like an unfinished erector set with bolts and holes and exposed metal jabbing our sides and ripping our shoes when we dared to reposition ourselves.

While two people sat up front in the seats, one to drive, the other to navigate and keep the driver awake, the remaining seven of us laid sardine-style across the freezing metal floors.

Smashed against one another, we shared our space with a handful of broken amplifiers, guitar cases, sleeping bags, and piles of wet shoes that, despite the freezing conditions in the van, slowly shed their slush and snow.

Arriving in each town, we would unload what gear we came with and set up on the floor of whatever venue the local area entrepreneur could afford to rent out. Veteran of Foreign Wars halls, church basements, community centers, dismal and dank corner taverns, we were not picky.

We would play because we believed in the words we screamed. We played because people told us we were no good. We played to emotionless and unresponsive kids because their eyes told us that we could not win them over. We played any place with an electrical outlet because that's what those who came before us did and now we stood with empty stomachs and broken strings in front of unimpressed crowds across America to put in our time and to earn our stripes. But most of all, we did it because we were nine egomaniacs who wanted nothing more than to shake and sweat and spit venom into the sky.

If you were with us, cool. If not, we had every intention of taking you out or leaving you with a scar, both figuratively and literally.

Our band was composed of five dominant and distinct personalities who refused to let our audience ignore us and you could put money on the fact that, at some point during our performance, one or all of us would dive into the folded armed crowd, feet or guitar first.

Those nights were our shots at freedom and independence. No overbearing parents, no oppressive bosses, no nagging girlfriends, and no expectations, we were the living and bleeding embodiment of youthful idealistic fury.

It was winter, conditions were harsh and barely anyone knew who our band was even in our own hometown, so on more than a few nights, it was merely a crowd consisting of the other bands' members, the promoter, and a few unlucky souls who happened to stumble into the wrong club on the wrong night to get warm, and were then assaulted by a handful of obnoxious kids screaming about revolution.

Our pay was minimal if even existent. Many nights, the amount of singles the promoter was able to hand over was merely enough to fill our gas tank to make it to the next town. Some nights, it was enough for food. Never was there a night for both, and hotel rooms were such impossibility that the mere mention of one for the nine of us to share was met with a volley of scoffs and punctuated with condescending chuckles.

Each night during our five song, twenty-five minute set, the singer of our band, panting frantically and sweating profusely, would look out at the sparse crowd in-between songs and ask empathetically if anyone could find it in their heart to let nine smelly boys sleep on their floor. Surprisingly, practically every night some generous soul would raise their hand. We never knew what we were getting ourselves into. Nor did they.

Late, after the show was over and we had packed up our guitar cases and second rate merchandise, we would slide our cold and sweaty and tired bodies back on to the floor of the van and pray that we could find a restaurant that was open before we rolled back to our new friend's house for our night-time homo-erotic antics. Most nights, since we couldn't load out our gear until the show was over, which was usually midnight or later, we wouldn't have many food options to choose from. Our running joke was, "Donut Dinner again," because in late night America it was Dunkin Donuts, and if we were in Canada it was Tim Hortons.

Many a night would we be ushered into a one-bedroom apartment where, like children shoving and racing to the front car of the roller coaster, would we call "spots" on the floor or sofa if one was available.

Once while in Indianapolis, while we slept in an unfinished basement, I made the mistake of falling asleep first and I woke to the sound of laughter. As I squinted my eyes open, trying to adjust to recognize figures in the darkness, I made out a white square quickly approaching my face. With cat-like reflexes, I raised my left arm to avert the object from falling on to my left cheek. Instantly, I felt a warm yet wet towel drool down my forearm.

"Dude," I said sitting up still wiping the sleep from the corners of my eyes, "what the fuck was that?"

Our singer and drummer, giggling like schoolgirls with their hands to their mouths, retreated back into the darkness.

"If this is," I grabbed the towel that was now adhering to me and flung it at them, "if this is what I think it is, I swear to God I'm punching you in the fucking face."

As my eyes cleared, I could make out the familiar milky-white fluid along with its distinct aroma. It was what I had thought it was.

"ARE YOU FUCKING KIDDING ME!?!" I yelled.

They ran to the stairs.

"YOU FUCKING CAME ON ME!?!" I yelled into the blackness, "I SWEAR TO CHRIST I'M STABBING YOU ASSHOLES IN THE MORNING."

But I didn't because by morning I had simply realized that

that was the consequence of being the first one asleep on a tour with eight other juvenile boys with no authority figure. You could get a small hand towel full of semen thrown on your face or you might wake up with a naked boy squatting over your head, eyes clenched tight in a desperate attempt to push out the tiniest of farts, you never knew. It's like when I was six and I was bitten in the arm by a rabid poodle because I had shot a cap gun in his face, I was never one to forget the lesson.

On one of our many gigs in Syracuse, New York, we managed to strike gold when one generous and very excitable fan approached and offered us a place to stay, not simply a place to lay our heads but an entire house to ourselves. The story went that it was actually a small house purchased by Syracuse University that was renovated into nine dorms where this dude's girlfriend lived. But due to the fact that it was Christmas vacation, all of the residents were back home celebrating the holidays with their families. Not only would we be unsupervised, but also we would each have our own beds, unbeknownst to the absent female residents.

As the door opened, we rushed up the stairs of the house with the frenzy and furor of nine puppies on a three-day diet of caffeine and crystal meth. Casting aside our luggage, we tore through each room, ransacking panty drawers, and overturning mattresses in a desperate search for sex toys and compromising Polaroid photos. But our looting came up empty; we assumed that the girls must have had a premonition that a gang of sex-crazed perverts with perpetual erections would be celebrating the birth of their Lord and Savior by descending upon their drawers of unmentionables with the worst of intentions. Not to be defeated, we picked up the discarded bras and underwear and began turning ourselves into sexy bitches. Red tops, striped bottoms, we sashayed down the hall like hirsute 60's Russian Olympic models. With all the femininity of drunken homeless men we laid on the beds with our hands behind our heads, exposing our unwashed underarm afros while asking, "Do yeeuw likee dis?"

Somewhere in the middle of the commotion someone stumbled upon a disposable camera that one of the girls had unfortunately left behind. We laughed and tried to out-sexy each other, "Make looove to the camera!" We yelled as we flashed away the remaining 20 pictures. Piling as many half naked boys in to her bed as we could, all while wearing her undergarments, would be the best holiday gift we could ever imagine. When the roll was finished, we returned it to the safety of the bedside table to be found and developed another day. The next morning we packed our clothes, climbed back into the van, and headed for Canada.

Night after night, we would coast into towns on fumes, load-in to the club, assault the audience with our sonic ferocity, then load back out and climb back into the freezing van. However, one specific night in Toronto stood out.

"Dude," our guitar player cried out from the co-pilot seat. "My friend from California just called and told me there's this totally fucked up place around here, it's above some Burger King."

"What is it?" I asked.

"He won't tell me, he said, 'Just go in and you'll see'".

And that was all we had to hear. We knew it would be seedy because the streets we were driving through were lined with prostitutes.

"So do you guys wanna go?"

"Fuck yeah!" We yelled.

It was around one in the morning when our guitar player said, "Yeah. This is the only Burger King around here."

As we pulled to a stop and slid the side door of the van open, pop cans and Gatorade bottles filled with urine fell to the ground and Dorito chip bags flew into the wind.

"So where is it?" I asked.

"I think it's up those stairs," our guitar player said.

Opening the door at the top of the stairs, we were taken

aback. I think that most of us were under the delusion that we would be walking into Sodom and Gomorra. Instead, a well-dressed woman casually sitting behind a desk greeted us.

"Hello and welcome," she smiled. "Have you gentlemen been here before?"

Someone blurted out, "No."

"Well, it will be sixty dollars a piece."

She might as well have asked us for a stack of gold bars considering how much we had been getting paid. A few of the guys bowed out and descended back down the stairwell but I was in for the long haul. The dimly lit office setting gave off the impression that it was a legitimate business but I couldn't help but get a feeling that shady dealings were going on behind her. Maybe it was the imposing security guards that flanked the doorway, or the heavy perfume smell that permeated the air, or maybe it was the receptionist's blouse that was buttoned one button too low. I looked over at our drummer, patted him on the shoulder and said, "Yo, lemme borrow sixty bucks."

The handful of us who remained were ushered down a dimly lit hall to a row of chairs that sat adjacent to a row of doors, as if we were sitting in detention in the hallway of a closed hotel. Nervously, we sat wringing our hands and began discussing back and forth about what could be behind the doors.

"Do you think they're hookers?"

"Man, I ain't banging no hookers."

"Just double bag it."

"Why would they be hookers when there are plenty of hookers all over the street?"

"Do you think this is one of those dominatrix dungeons?"

"Man, I get my ass beat by my moms enough at home, I ain't paying no sixty bucks to have some weirdo French Canadian chick talk shit to me and smack my balls with a paddle."

We came to an abrupt silence when one of the massive security guards in a tuxedo approached and said in a robotic and emotionless voice, "Gentleman, a host will take you one at a time into each room, there you will take a seat and you will be introduced to our girls one at a time. The host will return back into the room and you will tell him which of the girls you have selected." He hesitated before he turned to leave. "Behave yourselves, gentlemen."

Before we could turn to one another, a voice rang out from an open door, "Ok gentlemen, who is first?"

We stared at each other, mouths agape. "Ah, fuck it. I'll go," our second lead guitar player said confidently while smirking at us and disappearing behind one of the doors.

One after another, the host would open the door and usher one of us into the unknown room. I was visibly nervous, bouncing my right knee up and down and rubbing the back of my neck. I wasn't going to have sex with a prostitute, I told myself. But then what? What would happen if I paid for the service then backed out of it? Would she be offended? Would she laugh at me? The problem was, I wasn't sure what was behind that door. The only thing that kept me in that seat waiting for the host to open that door and usher me in was the fact that whatever laid behind that door was lewd and obscene. The two things that, for some reason, I found overwhelmingly attractive.

Ever since I could remember, I harbored an affinity for the raunchy and risqué. When I was four years-old, I somehow managed to evade my ever-watchful grandfather and bickering parents to sneak a local girl named Lisa upstairs and into my grandfather's bed where we took off our clothes and laid next to one another because that's the conclusion we came to when our parents had mentioned that our neighbors were "sleeping together". When I was in first grade, during a filmstrip where a dragon walked us through addition exercises, I coerced Stephanie, the cutest girl in the class, to hide under a table with me where she let me poke at her stuff and she poked at mine. And while I may have not had the ability to vocalize it, even at that young age I fell in love with the intoxicating feeling of being naughty and indecent. And that night in Canada, as I waited for the host to call me into a strange room, I felt that same rush I felt when I was four years old.

"Sir," the balding middle-aged host called out in my direction. "We're ready for you."

I walked over to him and he politely opened the door for me and sat me down.

"The girls will be with you in a minute. Remember the name of the one you like," he said as he turned around and walked out of a door in the rear of the room.

No more than five seconds passed when a tall, dark skinned, ravenous woman dressed in a studded leather bikini, draped in a white feather boa walked through the back door.

"Well hello, cutie. My name is Rachel, it's very nice to meet you," she said with a toothy grin and a wink.

I smiled timidly and tried to meet her eyes. I managed to hold her gaze for no more than two seconds before I had to look at the floor. She was so beautiful I was intimidated beyond belief.

"Remember my name, honey." She said as she turned her body before her head and strutted slowly out the door.

The next four girls were a blur. Name after name, I couldn't remember them all...until the sixth and final girl walked in. Brandy was her name. More comfortable with her surroundings than the rest, she was very casual with her tone.

"Hey," she said nodding at me like we had known each other for years. "What's up?"

Brandy had a thick and slightly condescending French Canadian accent and an air about her that said, "I honestly don't give a fuck if you stay or leave." I was mesmerized by her easygoing arrogance.

"Uhhh, nothing. You know," I responded.

"I like your tattoos," She said sitting down across from me. "Are you in a band?"

"Yeah," I said straightening up a bit.

"And where are you from?"

"Chicago."

With a dismissing wave of the hand, she snaps, "Ok, if you like me you tell the man."

As she retreats through the back door, the host reemerges. "So, which one do you like?"

I had to admit, I felt terrible. These women were paraded into a room with a drooling man where they were looked over, judged and chosen like cattle at a county fair. To think that six women were on the other side of the door, waiting for me to pass judgment. I felt terrible...but then the thought of seeing Brandy naked came into my head and my inner-dude came rushing back. I blurted out, maybe a bit too emphatically, "Brandy!"

The host walked out and Brandy returned to the room with a small bundle wrapped in a white towel. At an angle where I couldn't see, she unwrapped the towel and began laying the contents on a side table. I had no idea what was going on. She walked up to me and sat down on a bed directly across from my chair.

"So have you been here before?" She asked.

"Um, no." I said with an apologetic shrug of the shoulders.

"Ok, if you want to touch me anywhere but my face or my G-string it is twenty five dollars extra."

So wait, I thought to myself, is she or is she not a prostitute?

"If you want me to use a toy on myself its an extra thirty dollars and if YOU want to use the toy on ME its an extra forty dollars."

Still unsure of the direction this was going, I simply nodded as if I was reviewing for an upcoming history test.

"Ok, I will put on some music," she said as she stood and chicken walked in her six-inch white heels over to a white CD player where she pressed play and the sweet jams of some sterilized radio rock band echoed throughout the room. Brandy turned her head, smiled, and walked back over to the bed. She laid back and her eyes became heavy and her lips pursed like she was auditioning for a soft-core porno but she was blowing it by over-acting. She massaged her shoulders and rubbed her hands through her long blonde hair like it was an eighties metal video and she was the vixen blowing slow motion kisses to the camera.

Lifting her legs in the air and carefully gliding her fingertips along the lines of her calves, I couldn't help but think how absolutely cheesy this was. But as soon as I was about to lose hope, she took off her top. There she was, writhing on this bed in nothing but a G-string. I sat back in the chair and watched, half laughing at the hilarity of the situation and half excited knowing there was a naked girl in front of me.

"You can touch yourself if you like." She said in her best get-sexy voice, "Do you want to touch me?" She asked, innocently looking up from her contortion exercises.

Remembering that I had to borrow money from our drummer, I hesitantly shook my head, no. With an audible huff, she closed her eyes and proceeded to do her job.

Earlier, when I had walked in, I noticed a curtain in the corner of the room. I assumed this is where she would possibly disrobe but by this point, it obviously wasn't the case.

"Excuse me," I figured I would be polite seeing that I was interrupting her performance. "What's behind that curtain over there?"

"Ah, that's for old men," she said sharply. "You don't want that."

I got the impression she was trying to steer me away from it, so I pursued.

"Well, what is it?"

Slapping her hands down and throwing back her head, she sighed, paused while looking up at the ceiling, then jumped to her feet. She walked over to the table and started tearing open a package, I couldn't make it out but it seemed to resemble something red and made out of rubber. She then grabbed a

59

handful of rubber bands, turned around and pulled back the curtain. What she had revealed was a thin, door-sized wall of clear plexi-glass from the floor to the ceiling. The clear wall had been molded as if a female had walked into the glass and it cured with her outline intact. As if Han-Solo was frozen in clear Carbonite and had nice titties.

Brandy turned around and with the many rubber bands, began affixing the red rubbery thing on to a hole in the middle of the plastic. It looked like...a vagina she was strapping over the hole where I was told to insert my penis. She looked up at me and pointed to a large container that looked like the industrial sized ketchup bottles we had in the high school cafeteria. "This is here if you want to lube up your penis."

"Uh, wait," I said. "I don't have anymore money."

"Well, this service comes free with the room," She said while still preparing the machine.

Now it all made sense. She would have made more money by charging me the extras when she knew that I didn't have any knowledge of what was behind the curtain. She thought she was slick.

Motioning to the red apparatus strapped in tight on the hole with rubber bands, she said, "This is a brand new pussy, taken directly out of the package and over here..." she motioned to a black rubber blood-pressure hand squeezy thing. "This is to make it tighter or more loose."

Brandy walked to the other side and I stood in front of this imposing monstrosity still unsure of its capabilities.

"Ok, I'm going to turn it on."

Turn it on?

With the flip of a switch the room came to life, as if the chairs and the floor and the walls were buzzing. The air hummed and Brandy walked up against the glass, her body's curves conforming to the outline. I stood on the other side, our eyes were no more than inches away and we could see each other's naked bodies.

60

"Ok," She yelled over the hum, "Put your penis in the hole."

I pumped the gallon bottle of lube in my hand, applied it to my penis and as soon as I did what she told me I felt an immediate sucking sensation from the hole. Surprised, I looked at Brandy and she looked at me and smiled. I mean, it looked and felt as if we were having sex. Only we weren't. I was essentially, banging a wall.

"See that knob over to your left?"

I looked over my shoulder and saw a black dial on the wall.

"Yeah."

"Turn it to the right."

As soon as I turned it the room went from a hum to a loud buzz. It shook the paintings on the walls and rattled the doors on the hinges but most of all, it made the lubed up suction of the pocket pussy vibrate.

"Now fuck the hole." She demanded.

And I did.

The fact that I was a grown man, thrusting into a lubed up, sucking hole while simultaneously squeezing a rubber ball and turning knobs that not only made my penis vibrate but the walls and the floor too, this fact did not escape me. I looked to the floor and burst out laughing.

"Fuck it harder!" Brandy yelled through the glass.

And I laughed and squeezed and turned and thrusted even more.

I laughed because it was so ridiculous.

I laughed because it damn near tickled.

But mostly, I laughed because it felt like I was back in first grade.

As we walked back to the van, no one spoke much of specifics. We joked about the façade the waiting room gave, and talked dirty to each other in our best French-Canadian sexy accents, but we were all careful enough not to ask, "So, what did you do in the room?" Because some of us had girlfriends, some

61

of us were outright embarrassed and shame glowed on our faces, but most of us simply didn't want to give anyone ammunition to use against us.

That night, one of us came up with the infamous saying that came to be our tour mantra, "Keep it secret. Keep it safe."

Aspirations of the Couch Generation

ഇ෬൙

When the sun rose high over the surrounding three-story brick apartment buildings it would shine in through the large sliding glass door and light up the living room where I had fallen asleep the night before playing video games. It was the sun's blinding light and heat on those summer days that would force me from my slumber at no earlier than two in the afternoon each day.

I had become a human slug. A being that existed only to masturbate, eat pizza, and if I could muster it, work sixteen hours a week. I felt listless and sluggish, spinning my tires in the mud of, "Now what do I do with my life?"

I searched the floor for the TV controller amidst a sea of discarded, cheese-covered Taco Bell wrappers, spilled 44 oz. gas station buckets of Coca-Cola, year old Penthouse magazines, and dirty socks used as masturbation receptacles that were now stiff from semen. I cleaned off the remnants of a previous mashed potato fight stuck to the side of the controller, sat up, and pressed power. Immediately a commercial appeared advertising a job in the school bus driving industry. "Do you have what it takes to become one of us?" Asked the aging woman with the white granny afro.

I took it personally, "Hell yeah I do!"

"Well if you have a clean driving record you could become a licensed school bus driver."

"Dude," I said aloud as I rubbed my eyes and reached over to turn on the Playstation, "I could so do that shit."

I remembered the haggard, chain-smoking princesses who drove me around when I was young; retired mothers who, now in the twilight of their productive years, hated the world for the life they wasted. They were miserable. Taking their bitterness of the world out on a busload of young kids; we would get screamed at on a daily basis. "CHRIS! Sit the fuck down and shut the fuck up, or I will suspend your ass so fast your head will spin!" I would make funny spinning noises, twirl around, then fall back into my seat.

But I had dreams of being the cool bus driver, the driver who let the kids jump off the walls, have paper fights, and let the kids peel that old green gummy tape off of the back of the seat to put it in some poor random girl's hair. I wanted to be Otto from "The Simpsons" and Tom Hanks from the movie, "Bachelor Party" all rolled up into one. We would blast music and I would take the bumps at full speed sending the kids hurtling into the air.

Later that afternoon I called the phone number.

"Hello?"

"Yes, I'm calling about a school bus driver position, I was wondering if you had anything available?"

"Absolutely, we're always looking for responsible applicants."

"Yeah, I'm totally responsible," I said sarcastically as the clock read 4:30pm and I was still on the couch scratching my crotch through my dirty gray underwear.

"Well, come in tomorrow at 11am and fill out the paperwork and we will begin the process."

I hung up the phone with a feeling of accomplishment.

"Yo Boo, wake up." I yelled to my best friend who also happened to be my roommate.

"Fuck off."

"Dude, come on man, the sun is going down. Wake your punk ass up. I think I might be a school bus driver."

"Fuck! Off!" he yelled as he threw a dirty skate shoe that hit the door frame next to my head.

The next day I woke up early, showered, put on my best oversized GAP button up shirt (making my best attempt at looking respectable) and lumbered out to my car in the parking lot. I started it up, blasted the Van-Halen masterpiece, "1984" to wake me up, and sped away.

Arriving uncharacteristically on time, I parked my little purple Nissan amongst the giant Twinkie-like yellow busses and nervously walked up the stairs to the door that read "office". I pushed the glass door open and strode right up to the desk like the job was already mine. "I'm here to be a bus driver," I said with a confident nod of the head.

The silver haired woman behind the desk ignored me while she filled out a form of some sort. "Uh, hello," I said.

"Yeah yeah, I heard ya," she barked.

It doesn't take much more than being so readily dismissed to take the wind out of one's sails.

"Here," she said shoving a clipboard at me with a chewed up pencil barely hanging on by a thin gray thread. "Fill this out."

I smiled and she didn't even look. I took the clipboard and walked over to the seats.

"Name." Check.

"Age." Check.

"Birthday." Check.

The form was similar to all the other applications I have ever filled out in life. That was, until I got to the, "Will you be willing to submit to random drug screenings by hair sample."

Whoa, wait. You want to cut my hair?

"Will you be willing to undergo a background criminal check and be photographed and fingerprinted for the police database?"

Man, this was getting serious. But I thought, ah, who cares? I mean, I haven't been convicted of a felony and I've never even taken a hit off of a joint in my life, so why should I care? I circled, "yes" all the way down the list.

When I completed the form, I walked to the desk and

said, "I'm finished."

This was when she finally looked up at me, "Are you even 21?"

"Yes, ma'am," I said proudly.

"Don't call us, we'll call you," she said with a wave of the hand.

A week later, I got a phone call. "Mr. Gutierrez?" I thought it was for my father. "You applied for the position of school bus driver?"

"Yes, that is correct."

"You will begin your training on Monday at 7 AM, sharp."

"Wait," I swallowed. "Like, seven in the morning?!?"

"Yes, sir."

I was beginning to think this was a bad idea. I wasn't even going to bed, or let's be realistic, couch, until seven in the morning. But I thought about how awesome it would be to say to girls, "Yeah, I drive a bus. Awesome, right?"

That Monday I showed up excited to learn how to drive a bus. I was directed to go wait for the instructor next to the busses in the parking lot. Standing there surrounded by yellow busses, I couldn't believe I was actually going through with it. I thought to myself, this must be the way the little kids who had dreams of becoming astronauts felt the first day of their space training...well, maybe only for the kids who set their sights a little lower.

I was met in the parking lot by a very big and red-cheeked, no-nonesense looking man sporting an over-sized red and black flannel shirt. He had the trademark alcoholic nose full of burst capillaries, week-old gray beard scruff, and a red trucker hat that, from the looks of it, had seen many a drunken brawl. He was old, he was hard, and he had the hands of a person who handled a jackhammer for a living. He chewed tobacco and spit brown fluid before he said everything.

"Huh," he said spitting. "Well, lookie what we got huur."

Oh shit, I'm going to get pounded, or at the very least called a "rump-wrangler".

"Heehee," he cackled with a slight southern drawl. "You know earrings are for girls, right?" I laughed uncomfortably. I reached up and felt my ears; I had forgotten to take my earrings out.

"Yeah, my mom makes me wear 'em when I get bad grades."

I did my best at keeping it light, hoping that if I could get him to crack a smile maybe he wouldn't ride me so hard.

He gave me a good long look, squinted one eye, smiled and said, "I like you kid. Now come on, let's go learn how to drive one of these big bad motherfuckers."

He walked me over to one of the busses, put his arm through the window and released the door. We walked inside and he sat down in the drivers seat. "Drivin' one of these puppies is like drivin' ten cars, ya see."

I nodded.

"And you'll have the lives of fifty children in yer hands. So, PAY ATTENTION."

The next three weeks were a blur, if only because I was half asleep during the training sessions. There were written tests every day, rust inspections, instruction on how to repair the bus, and a fifty-point inspection process that had to be checked off every day even before I stepped on to the bus. I had to walk underneath the undercarriage and check for wild animals that may have set up living headquarters in the drive shaft, as well as learn how to handle diesel fuel. "This'll burn yer pecker off if you splash it on you, so don't play around and always use gloves." I had packets of take-home work. I had to study for my commercial drivers license. I had to make multiple trips to be finger printed, piss-tested, hair tested, and personality tested. At the end of the three weeks I was beginning to think this was far too much effort just so I could uncontrollably yell at little kids, but I was far too invested at this point.

The final week came and I passed my commercial drivers license test and my written exam with flying colors. All I had left was the driving test, which involved what I dreaded the most, parallel parking.

"Ok, see smart guy, you can do good on all those tests but when it comes down to it, you gotta know how to drive." I swallowed hard. "You knock over one orange cone today and you start from square one, you hear me?"

"Yes sir."

We commenced driving through the quiet tree-lined neighborhoods and I took corners with grace and style. I didn't miss a signal, I stayed within the lines, and I followed every rule to a T. I jumped zero curbs and made absolutely no sudden stops. I was gaining confidence and it showed in my face. "Don't get cocky, son," he said, as I tried to hold in my proud smile.

"Here, pull over into this lot." he said, motioning to a large empty gravel area. He pulled the door lever, picked up a box full of orange cones, walked off the bus, and through the side mirror I could see him strategically placing the cones on the ground. He walked back on the bus and looked at me sitting in the drivers seat. "See those cones I placed out there?" He asked. "Do not run them over."

Mouth dry, I said nothing. He reached in to his pocket and pulled out a spray-painted blue tennis ball. "And do you see this?" He held the ball up in-between our faces. "This will determine whether you pass or fail." He then stepped off the bus once again. I looked out of the driver's side window; he looked at me, held up the ball, placed it on top of the last orange cone and gave me the "thumbs up".

I took a deep breath, unlocked the parking brake, and began slowly turning the wheel to the right. Carefully, I scanned my right and left mirrors like I was taught over the past few weeks and I "trusted the mirrors" like I was told. Now, this was it, the big game. I eased in as far as I thought was safe, pulled the parking brake, opened the door, and jumped out.

Fast-walking to the rear of the bus I looked at his face. He wasn't smiling, he was staring. Staring at the orange cone. I approached him on his right side and looked down. The bumper of the bus was literally one inch from the cone.

"So," he said not taking his eyes off of the cone. "I suppose I have to pass you, huh?" He looked up at me and smiled. "Congratulations, son."

That afternoon, after much paperwork, I was instructed to arrive dark and early the next day at 5:30 AM.

Excited for my first day, I once again walked up to the silver haired woman's desk. "Well good morning," I was chipper. "Today is my first day, I was told to report to you for my route."

"Oh yeah." she said, unimpressed. "The new kid." She handed me a paper with a few addresses and dismissed me.

I was nervous walking toward bus number 11. This is what it all came down to. I had just spent three weeks of intense training and now I was about to experience the true power and magnitude of one of these big yellow bastards. After completing my initial inspection, I hopped in the driver's seat and started the engine. Busses were pulling out all around me. I lurched forward to get into line for departure. Then it hit me.

I didn't know what the fuck I was doing.

While they spent countless hours going over and over how to check for mechanical errors, the rules of the road, criminal background checks, finger printing, and parallel parking, they neglected to take the time to explain how the routes worked, supply me with a map of the neighborhoods or even discuss the protocol of picking up and dropping off the children. I began to panic. I wanted to run back in and tell them I wasn't ready, that I was going to fuck everything up.

But after everything, after all the time spent and the glares of condescension, I knew I couldn't walk back in there. I looked at the addresses again. They were corners of pick-up points. I thought back to the years I spent delivering groceries in these neighborhoods and it all came back. While I may have taken some wrong turns and approached from the wrong side of the street, I'll be damned if I didn't somehow get all of those kids to school on time that morning.

After my mild panic attack, I had a few hours before my next route so I chose to drive back to my apartment. I parked the bus across six spots in our apartment complex parking lot.

With my feet propped up on the railing, I leaned back in the white plastic balcony chairs of our second floor apartment and looked at the bus glowing in the morning sun. I made it. There was my huge yellow trophy staring at me. For a kid who had possibly the lowest expectations in life, this was, at the very least, proof positive that I could accomplish even the shittiest of goals.

I quit that job one week later. I had no intentions of staying and building a career there. More accurately, I had no intention of ever waking up when it was dark out to go to work again. I made that promise to myself over 10 years ago and I have yet to break it.

That afternoon when I called the silver haired woman to tell her I would not be coming back in, I realized it is good to have goals.

Even the shitty kind.

Skinny Fingers

ೞೞ

I drove ten hours in a car in a car with a girl I had a serious crush on to see a band. She knew I was crushing, I knew she knew it, and I prayed to Allah she felt the same way. I picked her up and traffic made a normal two-and-a-half hour drive a six-hour drive. I wasn't upset with this at all. When we arrived the band didn't even show up. I didn't even care. We stayed five minutes, complained about the heat and walked around the college town almost holding hands. On the way home she professed that she had a serious crush on me as well. We got a flat tire. I taught her how to change it. I got dirty and she wiped off my hands. As we drove home and I saw the city skyline get closer and closer, I drove slower because I didn't want it to end. She looked over at the speedometer, looked at me, smiled and held my hand. I pulled over at a train station because if I kept going it would have been the end of the day with her. I told her all I wanted to do was kiss her but I felt terrible because my friend had a crush on her as well. I held her face with my hands and I put my forehead against hers and I told her there was no place I would rather be on the face of the planet. She agreed. I teared up because she was the first girl I saw as my equal.

The Streets of Pamplona

ಐಂಬ

I hunched down to tie my shoelaces in double knots. I didn't come all the way over here to have something as ridiculous as a shoe falling off be the cause of my demise.

I touched the uneven cobblestone streets that have been host to this event for hundreds of years; I could feel that they were coated with a thin and wet layer of fresh wine and I wished myself good luck. If I got close enough to the streets, I could smell the sweet aroma of years worth of grapes. I stood up and looked up at the clock on the ancient building behind me, it read 7:30 A.M. I heard someone speaking English along side of me.

"Did you hear about what happened yesterday?"

"Yeah, it was insane. I saw him get hit. I don't think he saw it coming."

"The papers this morning said he was paralyzed from the waist down."

I turned and looked over my shoulder, "Hey, where are you guys from?"

The wide-eyed, dark haired kid who looked at me with a smile that distinctly said he was excited to speak to a fellow American answered, "Texas, and you?"

"Chicago," I said. "So you saw the guy go down?"

"Yeah dude, it was sick. He was in the ring and he didn't even see the bull coming, it got him right from behind. He flew up in the air like 3 feet and the bull smashed him again on his way down then he landed on his head. He hit the ground so hard that everyone in the stands knew that he was fucked."

"So you didn't do the run yesterday?"

"Nah, we wanted to watch it first," the dark haired kid said as he thumbed over his shoulder at his friend with the baseball hat and obnoxious sideburns.

"Dude, I'm so fucking nervous right now." Sideburns said to me with a trembling smile. I didn't have the heart to speak to agree, but to say that I was nervous would have been a massive understatement.

The day before, I had taken four separate train rides and a nail-biting hour-long bus ride along the steep cliffs of the Pyrenees Mountains just to get to the plaza in Pamplona, Spain where my feet now stood. All alone, I navigated the foreign lands of Western Europe in order to throw my life in front of a dozen wild and angry full-sized bulls and play the odds. Just like Ernest Hemingway had done 80 years before me.

Almost a decade earlier, I had watched a documentary on the Festival of San Fermin on the History Channel. The festival is a week-long annual celebration held in honor of Saint Fermin, the patron saint of Pamplona, which was popularized in glorious detail by Ernest Hemingway in his book, 'The Sun Also Rises'.

I wasn't quite sure how the Spaniards equated throwing yourself in front of an ill-tempered animal with paying tribute to a holy man, but I couldn't help but be inspired by their fortitude.

I used their wild and exhilarating tales of drunken machismo and the elation of staring death in the face and living to tell about it to motivate me to hop on a plane and voyage to what would be my Mecca. It is that "celebration of life in the midst of possible death" that drew me in.

The program also told the stories of those who did not make it, the ones trampled or gored by the sharp horns that spilled their guts on to the stone streets of Pamplona. I distinctly recall hearing a voice in the back of my head say, "You will never have the balls to do something like that." And that was all I needed to hear.

Immediately following the program, I turned off the television, pulled out a small rectangle of paper, grabbed a pen and began to write my "Things to do Before I Die" list. A list comprised of goals that I felt I was put on this earth to accomplish. No matter how insignificant or unachievable, I wrote everything down, folded the paper in half, and I have kept it in my wallet as inspiration ever since. Today was the day I was hoping to cross off what held the number one spot. Cross it off, or die trying.

I turned to my new Texas friends and said, "Ok, I won't lie. I'm so nervous my teeth are chattering."

Sideburns says, "YO, me too. Are your hands cold and clammy?" Without a word, I take my hands and grab his arm, "Ew dude, they're so slimy." We laughed in nervous agreement.

"When you hear the first burst of the firework in the sky, that signifies that they have opened the gate to allow the bulls on to the street," the dark haired kid said. "The second burst means they're actually ON the street. Yesterday it happened so quickly we didn't even hear the second burst, so just keep an eye on the movement of the crowd." This was useful information due to the fact that we were surrounded by thousands of people, jammed into the 15-foot-wide streets of Pamplona, all built before the invention of cars. Today these streets were jammed with thousands of drunken men from all over the world, here to test their will and tempt their fate. With the amount of people and the tight corners of the run, I figured we wouldn't even be able to see the bulls until they were practically on top of us, and even then, I couldn't imagine how I was going to actually "run" anywhere without trampling everyone within my path. I looked up and saw the clock read 7:45, I thought, well, I'll have answers to all of these questions in 15 minutes.

"Is it me or is this the longest 15 minutes of all time?" Sideburns asks. The dark haired kid and I laugh and agree.

"So, are you going to stay in the ring?" Sideburns asks.

75

"What are you talking about?" I reply.

"Well, the run ends in the ring with everyone pouring inside. There they corral the bulls then release two at a time to charge back in after everyone left in the ring."

"But can I get out of the ring?" I ask.

"Yeah, you just have to jump the barricade on the sides, but traditionally that is looked down upon. They see it as not having done the complete run and it is seen as showing a lack of manhood."

Shit. Not only was I going to have to run with the bulls, I was going to be held captive for who knows how long in a ring with a bunch of confused two-ton animals with foot-long horns.

"Yo, get to the sides, here come the cops," Sideburns screamed out as a group of cranky policemen come charging through the center of the crowd. "They're pushing the bulk of the people forward in order to thin out the crowd," He kept yelling.

"Fuck, this is getting intense," I say as I'm tripping over the men surrounding me.

"Dude, five more minutes." I hear Sideburns say to himself.

I look back up at the clock and it reads 7:57. The crowd begins to be overcome with an electric intensity. I could feel it in the air, like the moments before you know a fight is going to break out.

The chants become louder, "Ole', ole' ole' oleee'!"

The mass of spectators along the wooden fence barrier begins clapping and waving red flags, as the crowd begins to sway back and forth, knocking people to the ground as if we're all front row at a sold out concert.

I look to my Texas friends and scream over the mass hysteria, "Hey man, it was nice meeting you...good luck," and I give Sideburns a friendly pat on the back.

Swaying along and trying to hold his footing, Sideburns yells, "Yeah man, I'll see you in the ring. Remember, if you fall, STAY DOWN and keep your head covered, better to be trampled than be gored." Laughing, I can see him fall back into the crowd, swallowed by the sea of white and red.

Then it hit me, the icy cold shallow breaths. They overtook my lungs and for a moment the right side of my brain began to scream at me, "Dude, what the fuck are you doing?!? You could DIE here, this is totally avoidable!"

Out loud I yell, "Fuck you, I didn't spend thousands of dollars and travel half way across the planet to NOT do this. You hold your ground you pussy!" Luckily, the sounds emanating from the thousands of drunken people makes it so you can't make out a word of my frantic English.

BOOM!

Fuck. Was that the first...?

BOOM!

Oh fuck, the bulls are on the street.

My positioning and the surge of the crowd have pushed me a few blocks up into the course and I know that I have less than a minute before the bulls are right beside me. Before I can think, the mass begins to push me forward. Uncontrollably, I am forced to begin running or be trampled by thousands. My legs are barely touching the ground; I am kept upright by the surge of people shoving me forward. I begin to push and shove my way to the side of the street in order to get my bearings.

With my body tilted sideways, and following the flow of people, I maneuver through the rushing stream of white and red and grab a hold of the ledge on the corner of a building. I flatten my body against the wall so as to make myself as flat as possible in order to make room for the flood of the rushing crowd. I look to the building across from where I'm standing and it reads "P. Ghutuyi".

"Oh fuck!" I scream. I'm at what's known as "Dead Mans Corner".

This is the corner known for where the bulls all collide in to the wall because they are unable to make such a sharp right turn.

77

From legend, it is unwise to stand here because when the bulls slide and smash into the wooden barricade corner, they become disorientated and separate from the herd, making them nervous and agitated. They then get back up and attempt to trample the people standing closest to them. Which at this very second, would be me.

I turned to my right, to run, and there is a solid wall of people not moving, and just as I begin to panic there is a surge in the crowd. A surge unlike any I have ever seen. People are sprinting so fast in front of my face that I can't even make out shapes. It would be easier to swim up a waterfall or run head on into traffic. I would be instantaneously crushed and pulverized into the cobblestone by thousands in the mass hysteria if I were to try to merge into the onslaught.

In the distance I hear the CLOP CLOP CLOP.

My eyes widen and my mouth goes dry. I feel the blood leave my face, and my head and shoulders go cold.

Eventually, the flow of people slows to a trickle, minus a few sprinters looking backwards over their shoulders, necks contorted back, and eyes as wide as saucers.

As I turn my head to my left, I make out the image of a black bull running twice as fast as I have ever run in my entire life. My breathing ceases. Never has fear ever been so personified than at that very second.

I froze.

BAM! I watched as a bull, the size of a small car, crashes into the wooden wall that is Dead Man's Corner. Immediately following him were two others of the same size and stature. The first bull attempts to stand when two larger brown and tan bulls collide with him, knocking the first bull on its side.

I'm still frozen.

The world is slow and silent. I see the faces scream past my face and I can't take my eyes off of the muscles on the back of the black bull. I can see every muscle striation, how the hair lays on its back, the deep and dark gouges in the horns from past battles, and the glossy black eyeballs of this massive creature. My brain yells, "RUN! You stupid motherfucker!" But I can't. I'm so entranced with the sheer magnitude of power on display before me that I can't even think to exhale. I can't shake my eyes, like the moments before a car crash or a punch to the face when the alarm rattles your spine; my trance is pure and instinctual terror.

As if all at once, the five bulls stand and look my way. I am no more than eight feet away from terrified and crazed bulls that want to stab, gore, and kill everything within their path...and I am standing directly in front of them.

I slowly begin to shake my head back and forth to wake myself from the daze. A childlike panic fills my heart and my legs with adrenaline and my legs spring me into flight. Confused, I begin to run too fast for my body.

Instantly I fall to my hands and my knees.

"GET THE FUCK OUT OF MY WAY!" I scream, looking over my shoulder to the left as I see the faces of three bulls disappear, replaced with six-foot long ivory horns.

It is in these precise seconds when the seriousness of the situation dawns upon me. This is my life. There are very few moments when each and every emotion and action are pure and uncalculated. The occasions when we rely instinctively upon survival will be the defining seconds of our lives. This was one of those moments. And these are those seconds.

"GET THE FUCK OFF ME!" I scream as bodies begin to pile up all around me.

My feet push off of something that feels soft and it moves. I look between my legs and see a layer of grown men lying face down on the street, their faces smashed and contorted underneath everyone's shoes. People are using them to help get their footing and push off. Myself included.

For a moment, a wave of empathy overtakes me and I think about how in the face of this mayhem and chaos I should help these people. I'm in shock as the misery forces screams of agony from their mouths. I stick out my arm to help. But then through the mass I see the horns and the snout of three bulls beginning their charge. Directly at us.

The screams of terror that emanate from my lungs are girlish and shrill. The kind of blood-curdling scream that comes from your backbone and rattles your throat. I shove forward, and using my adrenaline-induced power to throw men like bean bags, I slip and fall again, and with my teeth clenched in horror, I claw at the shirts of some balding men in front of me, throw them to the ground, and power sprint my way through the carnage right down the middle of the street.

I am in a full-on sprint now, with very few people around me. As I look over my shoulder to locate the bulls, I see a man make a desperate attempt to jump through the large wood pillar fence that separates the runners and bulls from the spectators, only to be shoved, face first, back into the fleeing drunken and bloody mass by none other than a police officer.

This is no longer fun.

I'm not thinking about my list or how this will someday be an awesome tale to tell my friends back home; the fear that now grips me is making my teeth chatter and my heart beat so hard that my eyeballs feel like they are going to burst. Before I get the chance to let the tears of fright fall, I feel a hot wind pass my face.

Standing shoulder to shoulder with me are the three black bulls. Only two feet away are their horns, jutting forward like sabers, searching to impale the next person who makes the mistake of being too close. Searching to impale ME.

Like a spring, I launch off the street and onto the sidewalk. The combination of early morning air, adrenaline, terror, and sprinting have now turned my lungs to salt vapor and I am now desperately looking for a recessed doorway to hide from the bulls line of sight. Each one I pass is crammed with at least three people.

While the three black bulls have passed me, I am certain

that the two brown bulls have not passed by me yet, and it is not knowing where they are that powers my strides.

Eventually, I find a doorway with one middle-aged Greek man. I leap in the foot-deep recession and I press my body flat against the door. "Oh shit, here they come!" I yell to the man.

Here, I have a decent vantage point. I am on top of the incline of the street and I can see the hot breath of the huffing bulls as they run directly up the center of the street. I don't have time to pray, so I think: Dear bulls, please please do not see me and stab me in the guts with your horns.

With a 'whoosh' they pass.

I take a deep breath, smile, and say, "Well shit, you're not gonna live forever. Get in the game and make this worth it." And I jump directly behind the bulls, chasing them in the direction of the ring while nervously keeping watch over my shoulders for the bulls that are following.

Sprinting with them up the street I can see the massive hooves clomp and slide across the uneven stones beneath them, the people in front of them jump around like terrified rabbits, leaping against buildings and behind one another to make themselves less of a target, and I follow the bulls up the street.

The bulls run faster than I ever could and they lose me, but I still continue to run because I know there are still a few more bulls behind me somewhere. We round the last curve and with the end of the run just a few moments away, I look to my left and see the statue of Hemingway the city had erected and I say under my breath, "Just like you, old man. Just like you."

Following the crowd around the turn, I make my way down the street and into the dark corridor that leads into the stadium.

I am quickly approaching a pile of about fifty bodies, some limp, some bloody, most struggling to stand, but with the rush of thousands of drunken men running full speed, and twelve startled bulls, they don't stand a chance.

Using my small stature to my advantage, I bob and weave

my way through the unlucky, and run under the archway of the stadium. When I emerge through the other side of the arch, the light that before was blocked by the narrow alleyways immediately blinds me.

I hear the roar of the spectators in the stands.

I put my hand up to my face to shield the morning sun and I see every seat in the stadium is filled to capacity and every last person is standing and cheering us on.

I stop running, look down and note that I am now standing in sand.

I wipe the sweat from my brow and say, "Dude, you did it and you lived."

But I'm not done yet. I must still prove my manhood to this crowd. I'll be damned if I'm jumping any walls.

I do a quick body check to make sure everything is where it should be. Other than a few cuts, scrapes and bruises, I seem to be fine. But my celebratory mood is short lived as I hear the stadium gates slam shut, locking us in the center of the arena.

Many people panic and scramble to the sides, some and jump the five-foot wooden ledge and I realize, shit, this isn't over just yet.

Bull handlers with long green sticks soon corral the crazed bulls into a pen, and a cheer comes from the spectators. All of us runners look to one another and smile and hug each other. We congratulate one another on surviving this far, and we wish each other good luck. The mood on the inside of the arena is tense but calm as we wait for the two bulls to be unleashed upon us. A small group of runners has assembled at the opening of the corral. They sit, cross-legged, waiting. I look to a guy I hear speak with an Australian accent and I say, "What are they doing?"

"Man, those guys are crazy," he says, hunched over with his hands on his knees, panting. "They sit and wait there for the bulls to come out. It's like they're playing a game of chicken."

"Shut the fuck up, are you serious?" I say just as the

doors fly open and two bulls literally fly out of the pen, leaping, four hooves in the air over the maniacs sitting.

"OLE'!" The arena roars as the bulls go running wildly. Some of the men are trampled immediately. I rush to the side as the stampede rushes in all directions. While there is a significant decrease in runners, the arena is still packed. So packed that we can't see over each other, and while it wouldn't have been so much of a problem before in the streets because the bulls wanted to get from point A to point B, the bulls now have nowhere to go, nor are they with the herd; they are panic-stricken and nervous.

Runners surround the bulls and taunt them with red shirts or rolled up newspapers. The bulls make quick turns and run after the daring. Most people are quick enough to avoid the sharp horns, but some are not. I see a middle-aged Spanish man get cocky and slap the bull on its hindquarter. The bull snaps into action and drives directly into the man's knees, sending him toppling forward and onto the bull. The bull then throws the man upward into the air about six feet, and as he comes down, the bull thrashes its head upward once again, smashing its massive head and horns into the man's mid-section. The man falls limp in the sand. The bull then begins grinding its horns into the unconscious man's back and sides. It's an out of body experience. To see a man get smashed and gored and wasted in front of thousands of spectators whose bloodlust cheers this on is simply overwhelming. This is not fun anymore. This is not a sport. This is danger and horror, and I want out but my head keeps telling me, "This is what you wanted, now finish it."

So I stay.

They corral the first two bulls and release two more. These two are far more intense and agitated and quickly begin running circles around the ring. No one can keep an eye on where they are. There is so much confusion within the crowd, and people are shoving and yelling at one another. Anarchy sets in and people fall and get smashed from behind when they lose sight of the bulls. I stand, trembling in the middle of the ring, surrounded by the drunken mass.

We are all on guard, arms stretched out at our sides, ready to jump left or right like offensive linemen. I only know the bull is coming when the person in front of me knows the bull is coming, and he only knows when the person in front of him knows, and so forth. It is nerve-wracking, like when you're in a pitch dark haunted house and you know someone is going to come and jump out to scare you, it's the anticipation that kills you. This type of anticipation grips the back of my throat for the next 30 minutes.

Coming inches from death and injury. Full-sized animals with the capability of ending our lives are now erratically running circles around us while shouts from the crowd cheer us on. My nerves can't take it anymore. Then I hear it.

BOOM! The final explosion of fireworks, signifying the end of the run for the day.

A long and extended cheer roars through the stands and emanates from my dirt and blood covered brothers. A relief and happiness rushes over me that one can only experience when he knows he is out of harms way. I turn to my right and I hug a stranger. Then I hug another and then another. We are out of breath and we smell of fear and sweat and dirt, but we were in it together. All of us. Experiencing one collective and absolute emotion.

It was a test of pride, perseverance, stamina, and heart, peppered with mayhem and stupidity. But it was undeniable and it was an adventure that was now mine forever. I smiled at the crowd and raised my arms to the sun. The dust was still settling on my face and sticking to my sweat. I breathed it in.

The sweat.

The stench of animal.

The dusty arena.

The hearts of thousands of fools.

I wanted to remember this. This moment. This very second that I made this absurd dream a reality. I thought about what it took to get me to this very spot. To this sand covered floor in Spain. By myself. By my own accord. I thought about how life takes its shots and sends its armies of discouragement and procrastination to attack our lives so that we live safe and mundane. I thought about how, most of the time, those armies are victorious and I thought about how responsibilities and death and cancer and insurmountable odds prevent us from living with the vigor we so rightfully deserve. Because this world is ours for the taking and most people would rather live comfortable and discreet lives that don't make much noise or kick up much dirt rather than run into the burning buildings to save their own lives. I realized that this was one of the few times the sun shined upon my face and caused those armies to turn their backs. This time, I won.

I dropped down to one knee. I looked around at the faces I knew I would never see again, and I grabbed a handful of sand and shoved it into my pocket. I couldn't stop smiling as I walked out of the arena that day because I knew I had a handful of memories that no one could take away from me in my right pocket, and a list that now had a spot to be crossed off in my left.

Sex bitches.

Spitting venom into the sky.

I make girls pretty.

Make your mark.

In a sea of bro-hugs and high-fives.

I took this from inside the terror.

unbreakable.

STATE OF ILLINOIS   *GEORGE H. RYAN*   SECRETARY OF STATE

RESIDENT SCHOOL BUS DRIVER PERMIT
ISSUED:09-25-1996   EXPIRES:09-25-1997
IL DL#: ████████████ ████ SSN:████████

SEX:M   HT:5 08   WT:140   DOB:11-17-1974
SCHOOL BUS CLASS:B

CHRISTOPHER B GUTIERREZ
8127 WATERBURY APT-203
WOODRIDGE IL 60517

CHRISTOPHER B GUTIERREZ
NOT VALID WITHOUT SIGNATURE
ORIGINAL   3136818

DRIVER SERVICES DEPARTMENT

A bus driver diploma.

The Kings of the Suburbs

⚵⚴

Money has always made me feel uncomfortable. It gives me a false sense of security.

Growing up in a lower-middle class suburb, my single parent mother was constantly complaining about how she was worried that I would never understand the value of a dollar because I couldn't grasp the fact that she could only afford food and not the new suede Pumas I so desperately needed in order to look fresh on the dance floor. She clearly didn't understand how important it was to match your kicks to your Kangol hat.

As it turned out, she was right. I never truly learned to appreciate the value of a dollar. This was no more evident as when I had dropped out of community college for the 23rd or 24th time because I got the bright idea to hop in the van of whatever local punk rock band was touring, so I too would embark across the country selling t-shirts for five, maybe ten dollars a night. Sure, rent was due, but that shit always managed to work itself out.

See, I had a job working as an assistant manager at a video store for minimum wage. I didn't so much work there for the money as I did for the free stuff I could steal. I would work the grueling four-hour nights for $4.25 an hour, which after taxes worked out to about $12 a night, but I would offer to stay and close up shop. When left alone, I would load up my backpack with nutritious bags of candy for dinner, and while no one was looking, I could "liberate" the brand new video games that the next day I could take to a local resale outlet who would swiftly exchange them for rent money.

My plan worked flawlessly for months until the day I returned from a tour on the West Coast when received a call from a co-worker that I was going to be "let go" the moment I walked back into work. Word was, the owners caught on that things were "disappearing" during my shifts, but they couldn't get the evidence to prove it. So, they came up with the bullshit excuse that I was renting too many movies at one time. Nevermind the fact that I worked at a video store and was able to take them home for free, they were simply looking for an excuse to rid themselves of my thieving ass. While I couldn't blame them, I have always had the uncanny ability to justify my actions. I saw myself as a "Robin Hood", stealing from the rich to give to the poor. The rich being the family of owners who parked one of their three Lexus' directly in front of the store for all of us to admire, and the poor being my irresponsible ass.

The night before what was to be my final shift, I called to speak to the owners. Before they could get the words, "We're going to have to let you go," out of their mouths, I blurted out, "I quit." Thereby not tarnishing my flawless record of never being fired.

This left me not only without the means for ill-gotten funds but also without my paltry $100 checks for two weeks of work. Rather than be the responsible adult like the rest of my peers were, I figured I needed a new scheme…and that scheme came upon me by accident.

For years I had been documenting the Chicago hardcore and punk rock scenes by video taping practically every band that rolled through town. I had amassed a video collection of hundreds of bands over the years, and I soon found myself in a very fortunate position of peddling dubbed video taped concerts at local shows for ten dollars a pop. I had become "The Bootleg Guy". While I knew it wasn't the most reputable title, I churched it up by saying that I was doing promotional work for the bands by "giving them more exposure". Surprisingly, most of the bands that learned I was in the business of trafficking their illegal goods simply asked if I could mail them out a copy, because, essentially, I wasn't lying. I was pushing their little bands on kids new to the scene who, with pockets fat with suburban parents' money, were desperate to learn about what bands were "cool" and "up and coming". I just so happened to have my finger on the pulse of what the kids wanted. It's the direct result of having impeccable taste in music, what can I say?

Walking into each show with a stack of no less than fifty tapes, stacked neatly in boxes, I wouldn't even have the opportunity to set the boxes down before I was mobbed by hungry kids with ten dollar bills in their little paws. Ten tapes at ten dollars apiece were one hundred dollars. The same amount of money I made in one week at the video store.

Soon, I became a common fixture at shows, even taking requests for certain bands. I kept records and had to buy more and more VCRs to handle the demand. My bedroom in my apartment soon became a cluttered mass of wires, stacks of video recorders, and a mountain of blank videotapes.

I was a full-scale operation once the local independent record stores came calling. Agreeing on wholesale prices under the condition that they would purchase hundreds of tapes a month, I was set. No longer was I the shady character hidden in the back of the club keeping an eye out for the police, I had become the boss of an underground empire who operated by phone and was rarely seen in public with the evidence. Thousands of dollars were coming in monthly, enough for rent, food, clothes, and taking off and leaving with bands whenever I felt like it. I was back on my own terms.

My roommate Boo and I lived in a lower-class apartment complex. Most of the units in our building were allotted for Section-8 housing. In the Section 8 Program, tenants pay about 30 percent of their income for rent, while the rest of the rent is paid with federal money. Basically, we were the only people around who were too lazy to fill out the paper work for the welfare program. Large-scale gang fights were a common summertime tradition, as was converting the foyer of our building into a pressurized box of weed smoke. During the warm summer months, when our single wall unit air-conditioner wasn't doing its job, we, like most residents, would sit on our five-dollar white plastic chairs out on the balcony and survey the antics of the neighborhood while commenting back and forth with other tenants on different floors. One of our favorite characters was Vic.

Vic was a jolly white (well, actually more red than white) construction worker in his late 30s who sat outside on his white plastic chair from 6 AM until well after midnight slowly nursing "cold ones". Vic lived with a thick bleach-blonde woman who looked uncomfortable on anything other than the back of a Harley. We could only assume she was Vic's wife. While he told us he worked construction, we rarely ever saw him do anything outside of yelling at his "tramp" for more beer. His ever-present beer-belly covered in paint and saw dust implied that work was being done somewhere, yet we never saw him leave his plastic throne, not even when he urinated in the bushes.

Vic never wore anything but the same dirty pair of white short-shorts, and definitely none of that fancy stuff like shoes, socks, or a shirt. If available as an action figure, Vic would come complete with a case of Budweiser, two illegitimate kids, and "hand-to-mouth" alcoholic action.

But I think I'm giving off a negative impression of Vic. From an outsiders perspective, Vic looked rough, crude, and disheveled, as if life had rode him hard. Truth was, if you sat down for a few minutes and got to talking with Vic you would notice that the lethargic creature he projected was really in an exceptional and perpetual state of contentedness. If you took a second to look into his eyes and listen to his words, you would realize that Vic aimed low in life and his aim was dead on. While

94

billions of automatons rushed through this life with excess money in the bank, prescriptions for mood altering pills, and seemingly wonderful and productive lives, all Vic needed were his white chair, a beer, and a neighborhood full of hoodlums to keep him continually entertained. Vic knew the ins and the outs of the neighborhood; he knew when people came and went and he knew your name.

"Hey Chris!" He shouted at me one summer evening.

"What's up, Vic?" I said, carrying a stack of videotapes.

Laying back in his chair, he took a slow sip from the beer can, waited a few seconds to let the taste set in, "Ahh." Smacking his lips and without taking his eyes off of the can he said, "So, you off to make that money?"

"Yeah, if I don't drop 'em," I said, carefully navigating the sidewalk that ran in front of his ground floor apartment patio.

"Well," he said looking down the bridge of his nose, "I think I might need you to help me out with a little something later.

"Um, yeah, sure, whatever," I said, dismissing him.

Somehow managing to find my way to my car behind the tower of videotapes in my arms, I loaded in the tapes, hopped in to the front seat, started the engine, drove to the city, illegally sold my products, grabbed a veggie burger, and drove home.

Later that night, while Boo and I lay on the couches playing Crash Bandicoot until 4 A.M. I mentioned my run-in with Vic.

"Dude, what do you think 'a little something' is?" Boo asked.

"Man," I said, while cautiously navigating the character in the game. "What do I know? All I know is dude wants something from me and I don't want to get involved with his dealings. Nice dude, but shady dude, you know?"

"Oh, I know." Boo responded with a chuckle.

He laughed because he was a witness to the arrest when Vic had gotten caught with heroin a few months prior. I also called Boo downstairs to see the caved-in walls and smashed decorative wall hangings exposed on the night Vic mistakenly left his backdoor open for all the world to see the cave of filth he inhabited with his wife and her little boy.

The next day, after Boo had left for work, I was awoken early, around two in the afternoon, by a loud banging on the front door of our apartment. Jumping out of bed, rubbing my eyes and painfully yet carefully bending my morning wood back in-between my legs, I opened the door. Standing before me was a red-faced Vic, smelling like a four-day-old bar rag.

"Hey, remember the other day when I asked you to do 'a little something' for me?" He asked nervously.

"Uh, yeah dude," I said trying to keep my rager hidden behind the door.

"Well, I got this tape, right?" He said, coming in closer and looking from his left to his right. "And I know you have that bootleg video business."

"Um, I'm an independent band video distributor," I snapped back.

"Well, whatever you wanna call it, I need a dub of this tape. Can you hook me up?"

"Yeah, sure man. Why not? Come on in," I said. Who knows, I could possibly call in this favor in the future.

"Ok, here's the tape but there's just one thing," he said turning around and holding the tape up above his shoulder. "You can't watch it."

I looked at him confused.

"It's just...well, it's personal. Can you still do it for me?"

I thought this was a bit strange but I was still more than willing to help out a fellow scumbag.

"Sure, follow me," I said as I walked towards my bedroom.

"Ok, see I'll put in the tape here," I said to Vic as he was standing over my shoulder. "This one plays and this one records. I don't even need to see what is playing."

"Oh, ok, cool." he said with a bit of relief and amazement.

But what Vic didn't know was that I had an ancient full sized video camera hooked up to the Video Line Out on the playing VCR. This old early 90s video camera acted like an extra and emergency dubbing machine when I had a large order to fill. Luckily, that day it was plugged in and powered on.

As Vic turned to leave the room, I took a quick peek in the camera lens.

It was Vic and his little peepee.

And her.

And they were mashing privates.

Those two seconds are still vivid in my mind. Vic awkwardly positioned on top of his biker momma, bellies keeping each other at a distance while he jerked his body back and forth in a disgusting spastic display of attempted sensuality.

"Whoa." I said under my breath as I got up and walked out of my room.

Vic was sitting on the couch watching television when I sat down next to him and made awkward attempts at small talk. All I could think was, "Haha, I saw your wiener." For the next 20 minutes we sat and made comments about neighborhood gossip and Rosie O'Donnell's talk show.

"Yeah, I think its taped long enough," he said standing up. We walked back to my room where I stopped the recording VCR and ejected the tape.

"Hey man, thanks," he said as I handed him his copies and he turned for the door.

After Vic had left, I sat back down on the couch and laughed. I had just made a dub of a homemade porno for my downstairs heroin addict neighbor.

A few hours later, Boo returned from work.

"Dude," I said, jumping up off the couch." You will never guess what happened."

Boo and I kept each other constantly in the know of our

colorful neighborhood. When he was working, I kept an eye out for spousal abuse and gang fights. When I was working, Boo watched for burglaries and public displays of nudity. Sprinkle in some little kids chasing each other with roman candles and you would never need television again.

"Ok, so Vic from downstairs came over."

"Wait, VIC? The drunk construction worker?"

"Oooh yeah."

I began to tell Boo the story from beginning to end, putting emphasis on the fact that I saw his old lady naked. As my story came to an end, I could see a hint of disappointment on Boo's face.

"Wait, so you're telling me you didn't get a copy of this tape?"

"What could I do? I didn't know what was on it until it was recording, besides, Vic was lurking over my shoulder the entire time."

"Pssh," Boo scoffed. As he turned to walk away he muttered, "Total amateur."

We had friends over that night and as I recounted the events, they all seemed to respond the same way, "Dude, isn't this like, what you do? You're a scumbag bootlegger, you should always be prepared for a situation like this."

And they were right.

The next day, as I sat and watched Rosie O'Donnell, I heard a knock at the door. I walked to the door and opened it and again, it was Vic, holding the same tape.

"Hey, uuuh, you cut off the last like 10 minutes of the tape. Could you tape it again for me?"

I paused. I knew this was my opportunity. Think Chris, think. How do you do this? My mind wasn't quick enough to be put on the spot like this, I needed more time.

"Yeah, ok, cool. Not a problem, here's the thing," I said looking over my shoulder. "Uh, Boo is in the shower and sometimes he walks out naked, I don't want him to get freaked out if you're here. Could you come back in say, 10 minutes?"

Vic looked at me and I saw a bit of skepticism in his eye.

"Uuuuh, yeeeah...I guess so." I suppose any mistrust he harbored was eclipsed by the fact that he really wanted to see a copy of that money shot finale.

"Oh, and hey," he stopped, as he turned to walk down the stairs. "Is there any way you could make two copies?"

"Yeah, of course," I replied. Now why this dude wanted two copies of a tape of him having sex with his wife, I couldn't figure out. All I knew was, I wanted to be a part of it.

Immediately, I ran to my room, unhooked one of my VCRs, rerouted the wires so that it would record from the playing VCR, hid it behind my dresser, popped in a blank tape and hit record. Ten minutes later and right on time, Vic knocked once again. And once again, Vic followed me into my bedroom and carefully watched me set up his tape. And once again we sat in my living room, this time for a good half an hour talking about neighborhood indiscretions and daytime talk shows.

"Yeah, that should do it," he said, standing up. "I really owe you one for all of this."

"Don't worry about it, bro." I said smiling, knowing my copy of his debacle hid safely behind my dresser. "Just keep me updated on all the gossip."

"Will do," Vic said as he walked out the door.

Instantaneously as the door slammed shut I sprang off the landing and rushed to my room, ejected the tape, and brought it out to watch in the living room. I rewound the tape and pressed play. The recording was so seedy; I could see Vic hiding the camera behind a plant on the nightstand. Then, after a few minutes I saw Vic's lady walk in and get on the bed. The actual sex was soft and boring, and there was far too much excess flesh rolling around for me to get even remotely sexually aroused. Then I noticed something odd...Vic didn't have a mustache, not in the 6 years we had lived in the same building. Vic also didn't have a full head of bushy brown hair, and come to think about it,

Vic also didn't have an arm full of tattoos.

I suddenly realized it wasn't Vic. it was someone else. Banging Vic's wife. And for some reason, Vic wanted me to make him two extra copies of this tape. I never found out why Vic wanted two copies, nor did I ever hear about the tape again.

That was, until a week after I had dropped off a large order of videotapes at the local music store where I sold my bootleg videos.

"Is Chris there?" the woman on the end of the phone asked.

"Yeah, this is he."

"Uh, you know that batch of videos you brought in to sell?"

"Yeeeah?"

"Yeah, well, can you tell me why at the beginning of one of the tapes there is a homemade porno of two gross motherfuckers steamrolling each other?"

"Awww, shit. Are you serious? I am so sorry," I said frantically.

"Yeah, we put in the tape and walked away until some parent came running up to the counter, screaming, and we had to eject it."

"Oh man. I don't know what could have happened."

But I did know what had happened. After I had viewed the appalling yet oddly humorous display of filth, I had simply tossed the blank tape in my room and a week later when I went to tape a show, I had unknowingly grabbed Vic's secret porno.

A year later, I moved out of the suburbs and into the city. I left behind Vic and the madness of our quaint yet eclectically violent neighborhood. That year, I also sold my entire video "business" to someone who wanted to carry the bootleg torch. And along with the thousands of tapes I sold, I also slipped in a secret tape. A little present for someone else to find.

Damned

We walked past the brown wooden fence slowly, so as to not wake the Doberman Pincer. We got down low, despite the three o'clock afternoon sun beating down on us, and we walked quietly until we reached the spot in the fence where two boards didn't come together completely flush. A simple one-inch gap, and a vicious Doberman stood in the way of all that was holy to two eight year-olds. You see, beyond that one-inch gap lay a completely naked sunbathing blonde in her twenties.

On a blistering summer afternoon the week before, we had made the discovery, and now with a similar sun above we were going back with fingers crossed.

Smacking our grape Bubble-Yum and ditching our bicycles and backpacks behind a shrub, we got down on all fours and crawled along the length of the fence praying that the dog wouldn't get wind of our scent. We crawled and we smacked and our little veins pumped with their first surge of adrenaline and hormones.

There she was. A platinum haired bronze statue of perfection lying on an extended plastic lawn chair. Both of my hands were on the fence, framing my face. My breath was magnetized to her and I couldn't look away. I wanted to know what she smelled like, to touch her like the adults touched, to walk through the door and know she would be waiting for me and that she would be mine.

I was lost in my thoughts, in my fairytale daydream, when suddenly, the dog began to bark and the naked woman sat up and looked directly at me.

Mouth agape, hands shaking, smelling of purpley grape gum and crouching on my hands and knees was where I fell in love for the first time.

The cartoon "Voltron" was on the television when I got home.

I never forgot her, that episode, or that day in 1983 when I learned that all women were made of magic and possessed the ability to shoot butterflies in to my guts with a simple look of the eye.

One Night Stand

&ⱺ

"What do you mean you've never had a one night stand?" Josh yells at me with a flap of his hands. "How can you be as big of a fucking scumbag as yourself and never have had a one night stand?"

Sheepishly I say, "Man, I dunno. They always want to date me or something afterward, I'm not the one-night-stand guy."

"Well dude, you have a rep to protect. Let's make this happen tonight."

"How?"

"We're going to Riprocks," he says with an evil grin.

I knew of Riprocks. It was the suburban meat market. With a façade made up of simulated massive brown boulders, its bright neon lights sent out a welcome beacon through the crisp night air calling upon every insecure hairy-chested bro that possessed a secret desire to prove to everyone that they, in fact, did NOT have a small penis. Riprocks stood as a monument to gross objectification, and a church of white boy N'SYNC dancing. This is where the Cameros and Jeeps came to worship every Friday and Saturday night.

Oh, I knew of Riprocks.

"Dude, look at me," I said, staring down at my tattoos and once black, now ashy-colored band t-shirt. "Do you even think they'll let me in that place?"

"Trust me, you'll get in," Josh said, his face melting from an evil grin to a serious stare. "And no one who's ever walked through those doors and wanted to get ass has ever left dissatisfied."

I trusted Josh's word so I agreed but was hesitant to believe anything would ever become of it. Josh was a pro in this world and I was merely a tourist. Either way, something told me I was in for an interesting night.

Josh and I worked waiting tables at the same stir fry restaurant. That night I waited for him to finish up his shift around 11 so I could drive him back to his house and he could change into his club attire.

"The shinier the better," he said as he slid into the passenger seat, now wearing a pair of tight, black, shimmery pants.

This wasn't going to go well for me.

When we got to my apartment I rushed inside to find anything shiny and black. Rummaging through my closet of black band shirts I found a button up shirt and the only pair of black work slacks that didn't reek of stir fry oil. I looked like a cross between a waiter and a funeral director. I grabbed my lone pair of black boots that made me almost an inch taller, and I sprinted out the door.

Still buttoning up my shirt as I jumped in the car, I say "Is this ok?"

From his seat Josh gives me a smug look of approval and shrugs his shoulders. "Yeah, I suppose it will do. Is that shirt gray?"

"Come on man, it's old."

"Well, the club is dark, I suppose no one will notice," he says as I start the car.

As we pull out of the parking lot I begin to think, am I up to this? I'm going out with such malicious intent, there's no way I'm ever going to be able to pull this off. But I need to go. I need to feel out of place. I need to see if I have this in me, if I can be THAT dude. The one-night-stand guy.

I knew the apprehension was obvious on my face as we approached the infamous club. It was glowing amidst the dimmed lights of the Red Lobsters, Olive Gardens, and Hooters that encircled it. The parking spaces were alive and teeming with hordes of jock rockers and girls dressed in their skankiest outfits.

"Ok, just so you know, there's about a 40% chance of me getting my ass kicked as soon as I step foot out of this car," I say to Josh. "How do you think I'm EVER going to pick up a chick here?"

"Trust me, I know," he says with confidence.

And Josh does know.

Josh is in his early twenties with pimply skin, and is skinny almost to a fault. Complete with a vampire-like receding hairline he somehow manages to gel it into some kind of backwards-ass hipster hairstyle. He dresses well though, and always exudes a cocky swagger. Week after week, not too bright, but fairly attractive girls come in to our restaurant and ask Josh when he's going to take them out. He tells me he's far too smart to spend money on girls, he tells me that he "leaves that to the suckers."

He seems to do well with this game. He's creepy, smarmy, and obvious. He's touchy and feely but he has this move that always seems to work.

"Want to see the master in action?" he says to me one day at the restaurant.

In disbelief I respond, "Yeah, I want to see this 'move' you're always talking about."

I hang back and watch from the kitchen as he walks up to a round table of six middle- aged soccer moms. He begins with regular waiter chatter. They don't seem very receptive. But he's persistent. He begins telling them stories, making them laugh. I can see their body language change indicating they are becoming more comfortable. They run their fingers through their hair and when they smile they cover their faces like bashful teenagers. Josh was in.

Then I catch it.

The move.

He turns his shoulders slightly, lowers his head as if he's putting his chin in to his chest, closes his eyes, then begins to slowly raise his head to them at a 45 degree angle and while smiling the cutest 4 year old I-just-ate-all-the-crayons grin, he opens his eyes really wide and says, "Now, would any of you ladies be interested in buying some dessert?"

I see it. The women melt. They are in the palm of his hands.

Josh was notorious for being able to up sell anyone ANYTHING, and that's how he did it. So when he told me to trust him, I did.

We open the doors and step out of the car and I feel a buzz of electricity in the air. I'm surrounded by bros wearing transparent mesh black shirts and girls in riding boots with hand towels for skirts, their eye shadow obviously applied with a paint roller.

I am out of my element. I know it. Josh knows it. The surrounding meatheads and skanks know it. But no one's had any alcohol so the energy is still positive and non-threatening like the first hour of a high school kegger.

We walk to the door and we stand in line as a ridiculously large man on loan from the local professional wresting team grabs my drivers license and scrutinizes it as if I'm eight years old and trying to gain access to the local titty bar. He hands me back my identification, looks me up and down, chuckles and says, "That'll be ten bucks."

I had just seen him let the group of skanks in before me and they didn't hand him shit. Then I remembered I didn't have boobs and Fuck Me boots on.

I handed him ten dollars and he waved me in.

Inside we immediately walk to the bar to scope the scene. I order a Sprite, no ice, Josh orders a vodka tonic.

I look around. There are two separate areas. One is for the bar, well lit, with video games, darts, and loud, radio-friendly music. The other is off to our right, down a dark corridor that leads to a smoky room thumping with techno music.

A weather-beaten and leathery woman with serious cleavage and a faded green rose tattoo on her left breast leans over the bar and says, "That'll be ten dollars."

"Ten bucks?!?"

"Yeah, six for his, four for yours."

A four dollar 8 ounce Sprite. I think to myself, some government agency should really look in to this.

"Ok dude," Josh says. "Right now we're getting our bearings. Give it a few minutes and we'll head into the dance club."

What am I doing here? They're all going to figure me out. In one second the music will screech to a halt and the DJ will say, "Um, this is our scene and we know what you're doing here. Beat it, skinny, or the dudes with the chest hair and gold chains will have their way with you."

I begin to think of excuses I can tell Josh to get us out of there, when he grabs me by the arm and yells, "Whoa, look at those chicks!" He points toward a small group of girls who are just engulfed by the smoke of the corridor. "I'm going to go dance with them," he says.

And just like that, he was gone. The kid had balls, even if he wasn't all that physically attractive, he had balls. Leading me like a reluctant child toward his first day of school, Josh grabbed me by my shirtsleeve and pulled me into the darkness.

The combination of the dark and mysterious corridor and the oily sent of artificial smoke machines brought to mind local haunted houses. That is until I am blasted in the face by pulsating green lasers. I wave my hands in front of my face and once the smoke clears I see hundreds of scantily-clad, barely-legal girls attempting their best seductive dance moves along to the techno that was thumping through my chest and an equal number of hair-gelled boys leering at the dance floor like wolves salivating over sheep in halter tops.

"Hey, I'm going to go find those chicks...You gonna be ok by yourself for a while?" Josh says over his shoulder as he walks away.

"Yeah dude, I'll find you." But Josh had already been consumed by the dense smoke, thundering bass, and criss-crossing laser beams.

I walk around to where it's the darkest. I need to take this all in.

In the center of the room is an octagon shaped wood dance floor, and in the middle of that is a platform about three feet high. On the edges of the dance floor are three winding staircases that lead up to six foot-tall black metal platforms that resemble back-alley fire escapes. Encircling the dance floor are ledges; I assume these are intended for drinks to be set upon, but each and every available spot is now overflowing with dudes. Guys leaning on their hairy and muscular forearms, trying their best to eye-fuck every unsuspecting girl who makes the mistake of looking their way. Behind them and along the far wall are a few booths where couples make out under cover from the lasers. Close to me is another bar with stools.

I walk up to the bar.

"Sprite please, no ice."

Eight dollars down, I walk slowly like I have somewhere to be on the outskirts of the dance floor.

No one looks at me. No one.

In one way, this means I haven't been discovered as an intruder. I'm beneath the radar, but also off the radar of any potential girls.

There are a few guys dancing with girls. They look ridiculous. I watch them and put my fingers in my ears and picture them without the music. Ridiculous. While ironic fun, I find the idea of dancing to be absurd. Tonight does nothing but prove my point. The boy band rejects, complete with stereotypically flamboyant link-chain necklaces and sweat dripping down their faces, flail across the dance floor like wounded epileptic rabbits. With choreographed moves straight out of teen-pop videos, they seem to go over well with more than a few stumbling, yet attractive girls. I think, if this is what it takes to compete in this arena, I'm done for.

Squinting to make out figures through the dark, I see one Justin Timberlake wannabe dancing with two blondes and one brunette. One is clearly humoring him, and from the other girl's body language, it's obvious they want him gone. I smile and laugh. The guy turns and sees me smiling and begins walking toward me.

"Dude, I told you I was gonna dance with 'em," Josh says, smiling ear to ear.

"Good job, brah," I say with a slight twinge of condescension.

While the girls may not have been very receptive to his advances, I couldn't knock the balls on the kid.

"Ok, we need to find you a chick," Josh says, scanning the dance floor. "You need to go out there and dance."

I look to the floor, smile, and shake my head back and forth. "Are you fucking kidding me?"

"Well, no chicks gonna notice you standing there holding up the wall."

True.

"Listen, just keep the beat and walk up to a group of girls. If one wants to dance, she'll turn around," he says like a true instructor.

"Fine, but don't watch me. I look pathetic when I dance."

"Ok, I'll find you in about an hour when the place closes," he says as he dances his way back to another unwary group of girls.

I come to grips with the fact that fortune favors the bold so I take a step onto the wood dance floor. No one seems to notice. I start nodding my head. No one notices. I start moving my shoulders, my hips, and my feet, careful not to flail too much or be mistaken for a spazz. I observe the guys who are trying too hard to impress and the girls who watch them laugh and cover their mouths. I'm afraid I would leave in a screaming woman-like frenzy if that happened to me, so I keep it subtle, subtle enough to blend in but just not enough to stand out. A solid B−, C+ performance.

I dance my way over to this brunette I've had my eye on since I walked into the room. I'm standing behind her doing my dance-but-not-dance.

Notice me.

I can only assume she gets the I-have-a-feeling-someone's-standing-right-behind-me feeling when she looks over her shoulder, stares me up and down, gives me a friendly smile, turns back around and continues dancing with her friends.

Ouch.

Ok, lets try this again. Remember: smile, keep the rhythm, no arm flail, be subtle, don't look like a creep...wait, do I look like a creep? I'm alone, clearly an amateur in this realm...am I THE creep?!?

Ok, calm down. You're doing fine, no one's pointing and laughing...yet.

I scope out another couple of reasonably attractive girls. Ok, there we go. Smile. Subtle. Think smooth. Think Eric Estrada CHIPS era. I slowly come dance up behind the cute blonde, she looks over and smiles, I smile back with my eyes, her friend looks over, she smiles, I smile back. For an instant we're all dancing together. Keeping the beat together.
Smiling together.

Wow, this is what this is all about. Not the dancing, but the connection. I feel their approval and I like it. I feel desired. Until a slow moving, hulking man comes walking up to the girls and hands them drinks. He looks at me and gives me the whatsup nod. I smile and give it back. But it's too late; he has their attention and has strategically muscled his way into my spot. The girls' attention is not mine anymore. I feel my shoulders begin to slope. Defeat. Hold it together, Chris, slowly retreat back to the open spot at the ledge.

I set up shop at the ledge. It's getting late and the crowd is thinning out. Everyone is noticeably drunk. Sloppy tongue-to-face make outs are all around me, girls are falling from the platforms and everyone is spilling their drinks. I relax and take it all in. The lights, the music, the thrill of the hunt, the smell of sweat and alcohol, it's all so overwhelming. I've thrown in the towel. I'll wait here until Josh finds me. I begin scanning the floor for my friend when I notice someone staring at me. She's short, blonde, and moderately cute like she was the attractive girl next door in high school but one too many six packs and early morning community college classes have had their way with her body. But she's staring at me with these eyes that say, "You're mine."

It's a strange feeling. While I may have be able to con a few girls into my bed, no one has EVER given me the I'm-going-to-fuck-the-shit-out-of-you eyes. I'm just not that dude. I look over my shoulder to make sure she's not directing it at some slick looking crotch rocket-driving greasy-haired boy. Nope. She's staring right at me.

Seal the deal, Chris. Make her know you want exactly what she wants. What should I do? Wait. Do Josh's move, the head down thing with the eyes, do it quickly before you lose her.

I lean forward a bit more on my elbows, I tell my body to act cool, I pucker my lips and clench my teeth together to make my jaw more prominent in the best blue-steel-Zoolander face I can make, I let my head drop, I look from side to side, and when I lift it I open my eyes wide and smile directly at her. I let it sink in. One second, two seconds, three seconds. She knows I am staring at her. Four seconds. This feels awkward. Five seconds. Don't panic, don't panic. I begin to panic. Look away. Look away. Six seconds. I mouth the word "hi." Seven seconds. My eyes turn away, my head follows.

I feel seriously cool. I've never been so bold and obvious in my life with a girl. Please let this work. Please. I give it a few seconds and I look back. She's gone. Well, that's three for three tonight. I tried. I guess I'm NOT that dude. Time to lick my wounds, find Josh, and retreat to the comfort and familiarity of Internet porn. I grab the glass that held my four-dollar Sprite, stand up straight and turn my body toward the bar. Just as I begin to take the first step I feel a hand on my waist. "Hey, where are you going?"

I look down. It's HER.

Her eyes are heavy with blue eye shadow and she has a grin that curves more to the left than to the right. She waits for my reply.

"Um, I was just going to the bar to drop off this glass."

"You weren't going to wait for me?" she says with pouty lips.

"I thought you had left."

"I am going to leave soon, it looks like the club is closing."

This is it. This is my window. Take it. Take it.

"So..." I say, clearing my throat. "Um, what are you doing afterwards?"

I feel like I'm standing on the ledge of a window, like I'm on thawing ice, like everything coming from my mouth is transparent and my intentions couldn't be more noticeable.

She knows what I want. She knows. I see it in her eyes. She knows.

"Noooothing...what are YOU doing afterward?"

Oh she knows.

"Um…" Think, Chris. "I'm going to have people over at my apartment, would you like to stop by?"

"Of course. I'll tell my girls I'm leaving," and she walks away.

Ok. Don't freak out. You know you just lied to her; no one's going to be at your apartment. It's just going to be me, Josh, her, and the cats.

Just then, Josh finds me.

"Dude, I saw that chick talking to you. What's going on?"

"Well, apparently she's coming over to my apartment."

"Are you serious?"

"Yeah. Um, I told her I was having people over. Would you mind rolling past my apartment for a while just so I don't look like a total liar?"

"So let me understand this," he says, shifting the weight in his hips, "you want me to stop by your apartment while you make out with some random chick that you'll probably never see again just so you don't look like a liar? Here was his protégé making progress and the master was striking out. His ego was taking a beating.

"Please? I don't know how this is going to go."

Josh can see the nervousness in my eyes. He looks at me for a second.

"Fine." Then, slowly, Josh's face lights up with excitement. "Hey, wait. Do you think she would be down to have a threesome?"

"Man, I don't know. I've had all of a two-minute conversation with her. How would you even instigate something like that?"

"I don't know. But I know they happen."

"Well, let's just see how this thing goes."

I look over and I see her walking toward me. "Ok, I told my girls. I'm going to follow you in my car. Is that ok?"

"Yeah sure," I smile, trying to contain my excitement. "Oh sorry, this is my friend, Josh."

"Nice to meet you Josh, I'm Jenna," she says, extending her hand.

"Nice to meet YOU," Josh says, taking her hand and creeping her out a bit.

We leave together, Josh and I to my car, Jenna to her small blue Dodge Neon.

The ride home is fast, the excitement and what the night holds make me run red lights and speed though sleeping neighborhoods.

We arrive at the parking lot of my apartment around 1:30 A.M. Jenna pulls in along side of us. She follows us inside. I open the door to my apartment and it's a mess. I never actually believed I would be bringing anyone home from a club tonight or ever for that matter. I apologize, and she either doesn't care or doesn't notice. Jenna and I take a seat on the sofa. Josh sits on the love seat directly next to us. We do not turn on the TV.

"So, I don't know if anyone's going to show up tonight," I say.

"I don't care," Jenna says, looking up at me and smiling.

Awkwardness fills the air. I don't know how to begin the make out and I certainly don't know how when there's a silent and smiling creepy friend of mine scrutinizing every move I try to make.

"Oooh, my hands are cold," I say, rubbing them together.

"Here, put them under my shirt."

Whoa, this is going to happen. My mouth goes dry and I cough.

"You ok?" She says, and starts leaning in to kiss me.

I close my eyes and say, "Yes, now I am." It comes out as cheesy as it sounds, but Jenna doesn't care.

We begin making out. My hand is still lumbering up her shirt. I re-adjust. She leans back and pulls me on top of her.

Outside of the average make out sounds, the apartment is silent. I open my left eye and see Josh only two feet away watching like a cat ready to pounce on a mouse. He's sitting there in his shiny black pants with his hands clasped in his lap leaning forward as if to judge each and every tongue technique.

I try to ignore it.

Jenna takes off her shirt.

We make out more.

Jenna stops, looks at me and whispers, "Um, can you tell him to go somewhere else?"

Despite being directly next to me, Josh overhears.

I see the disappointed look wash across his face as I ask, "Josh, can you go in the other room?"

He sits back, his face crinkles up and he says, "Fine."

Josh jumps off the couch like a spoiled little kid who has been denied a birthday party. As he's walking away into my bedroom he gives me the finger and smiles.

Jenna and I continue.

More shirts come off. Socks come off. Soon, all clothes are off.

Twenty minutes later, Jenna and I are having very average sex on my couch. This certainly isn't how I expected a one-night stand to be. I expected more heat and passion and intensity. All of which are exactly what's lacking. I'm having sex on my couch and I'm bored. I think to myself, I can't wait 'til she leaves so I can masturbate. But then I think to myself, maybe we can spice things up a bit.

"Hey," I say while thrusting. "Would you mind if Josh came out and watched?"

"At this point, I don't care," she says smiling.

I push myself up on my hands and knees, stop thrusting and yell, "Yo, Josh!"

No answer.

"JOSH! Yo, you can come out here if you want."

I wait a few seconds. No response.

Just as I look down at Jenna the door to my bedroom begins to slowly open. The lights aren't on, which I find strange. Josh walks out of the room.

My jaw drops.

Josh walks toward us wearing no pants, black socks, a half unbuttoned white dress shirt, and sticking out from the bottom flaps of his shirt is a bright-red and glistening hard-on which he is stroking like a mad man. There is no smile on his face. He is all business. He goes back to the love seat and begins masturbating like a wild chimpanzee. I can't contain myself and I begin to laugh. I laugh at the look of determination on his face, I laugh at what he's wearing, and I laugh at the ridiculousness of the whole situation.

Jenna looks at Josh and smiles. So I continue.

After about five more minutes she looks at me and says, "Um, I have to pee."

"What?"

"I have to go pee. I'll be right back." She rolls her naked body off the couch.

Josh walks over to me, red and shiny hard-on still in hand.

"Yo, you think I can join in?"

I can't handle Josh standing over me having a conversation with his dong in his hand, so I stand.

"I don't know, dude, she doesn't seem very into the idea," I say, while trying to maintain my own hard-on.

"Dude, come on, ask her."

"No dude, you ask her."

We are grown men standing two feet from each other, stroking our dongs, trying to figure out how we can ask this girl if we can have a threesome.

"Shhh, shhh, here she comes."

"Ok, are you gonna finish up?" she says to me as she lies back down on the couch in the missionary position.

"Um, do you want me to?"

"Yeah, I have to get up early tomorrow," she says, as if she is merely asking me to turn off the television or take out the trash.

I begin trusting again.

I start laughing, she doesn't notice. I look over to Josh. He's mouthing the words "Ask her. Ask her."

I mouth back, "FINE!"

"Um, hey, would you mind if Josh joined in?"

Her eyes open. Her head cocks to one side. Her eyes squint and with complete and total conviction she says, "Are you fucking kidding me?"

I snicker.

"Haha, nah, it's cool." I say trying to keep the mood light, "I figured couldn't hurt to ask, right?"

"Well, no."

I bury my face in my chest and continue to thrust and laugh. I look over at Josh and he looks as if someone just let the air out of his tires. He gives me the finger again. Then his face changes like he just remembered something. I keep thrusting and look over. Josh seems to be pondering something. I'm thrusting, but I'm watching his face. Josh is looking intensely at the ceiling. I'm thrusting. His eyes drop from the ceiling to mine. I'm thrusting. He smiles. I'm thrusting.

"Poooooot."

Josh lets out the loudest, wettest sounding fart I have ever heard, only two feet from both of our heads.

I stop thrusting.

Josh smiles.

I can't control it anymore. I laugh out loud.

He looks at me again with a you-son-of-a-bitch face, his body lunges forward and I hear it again.

"POOOOT!"

"POOT!"

It's the sound of a muffled duck coming from inside the couch. Each fart is shorter and shorter, until Josh can't push out any more. Finished, he smiles, looks at me, nods his head and retreats to the bathroom.

"Uh, did he just fucking fart?" Jenna asks with a bit of hesitation.

At this point I can't control my laughter even though I'm still inside her. "Uh...haha...yeah."

Putting her hands on her head she says, "Wow. This night is a first."

I sit up and look down at my deflating penis and say, "Yeah, you could say that."

A Picture is Worth a Thousand Words ...Most of them Lies

෨෬

"So what are you doing tonight?" She asked me on Instant Messenger.

"I just got in from watching some shitty bands, I'll probably just sit around tonight. Why?"

"You wanna make out?" She responded with an internet smiley face emoticon.

We had been flirting on and off for a couple months after lurking each other out on the infamous capital of online creepery, MySpace.com. We exchanged emails, she said I was cute; I said she had nice boobs. So I gave her my Instant Messenger name and we began to talk sporadically online.

She was just cute enough, from what the handful of strategically taken MySpace pictures would show, and I was just vulnerable enough after getting out of a long-term relationship that had recently fizzled to a close. "Yeah sure," I said. "Why not?"

"Ok." She proceeded to give me directions to her apartment. "Give me 23 minutes to shower and text me when you're downstairs in front of my building, the buzzer is broken so I have to take the elevator down to open the door and let you in," she typed.

And that was the simple conversation that set into motion the events that were to transpire that evening. If I could have possibly known what lay in wait for me behind that door I would

119

have erased her name from my buddy list and never looked back. But I was taking a chance; I was meeting up with someone I had never met face-to-face, or spoken with on the phone, for a "make out" date. I loved the idea of spontaneity. I loved the randomness of taking a chance and the seediness of the entire proposition. I was completely unaware of what she looked like or smelled like or tasted like. The idea of going over to make out was so anonymous, so completely hedonistic. It was like a mini-adventure, a vacation from the droning mediocrity of coffee dates and over-priced club cover charges. I was so in. It was perfectly filthy.

I relaxed, turned off my computer and said aloud, "Man, this is awesome."

It felt refreshing to not have to put on my front of cool and aloof. To be so comfortable in my sexuality that I could have a "make out meet up" and not expect anything else. It was straight to the point. No dinner, no hand holding, no small talk, and no qualifying myself to her.

I walked out of my room and into the bathroom to take care of all the necessary obligations before "meeting with company." Wash my face, brush my teeth, powder my balls, it was all standard by this point. I put on my shoes and walked out the door to hail a taxi.

Jumping in the cab I told the driver the address and settled in for a 5-minute drive. "So guess where I'm going?" I said into my phone while sitting in the backseat.

"Um, probably to meet up with some dirty skank," my friend Gheesling replied.

"Hey, come on now. She might be a really nice lady," I said holding back a chuckle.

"MIGHT? What, you mean you don't know her?"

"Um, well...I mean, I sort of know her. We have been talking on the internet for a couple months now."

"Dude, you are filthy," she said. "Ok, go have fun and call me afterwards and tell me how it goes."

"Always." I hung up.

"It'll be $6.50, sir," the cab driver yells over his shoulder. Little did I know it would cost me much more than that.

I stepped out the door and on to the sidewalk. The sun was setting in the warmth of a late spring Friday. I looked both ways before crossing the busy street and casually sent a text to the mystery girl stating that I am downstairs in front of her apartment.

"I'll be down in a couple minutes." She replied.

Standing at the entrance to her apartment building I find I'm a bit antsy, I can't keep my hands still so I shove them in my back pockets in a vain attempt to look cool and collected because I am anything but. Nervously, I bounce around from foot to foot. I can feel my heart rate spike and the "I have eight kittens moshing in my stomach" feeling coming on. "Slow down, dude," I say to myself. "She's just a girl. She's just a girl." A woman comes to the door and I hold it open for her. "Thank you. Do you need to get in?" She asks.

"No, no thank you. I'm waiting for someone," I reply.

A few more minutes pass and another woman comes to the door and I hold it open for her. "Hello," She says.

"Hi," I say as I turn away from her.

She stops, looks at me and says, "Um, Christopher, right?" The expression on my face couldn't have read anything but, OOOHH FUUUCK.

She was standing before me looking NOTHING like what the pictures had represented. She was a walking, talking, internet horror story. You know the kind of, "Well, what if she's an axe murder?" or, "What if she's nasty?" or, "What if she's using 10 year-old pictures?" That kind.

In her pictures she had beautiful shoulder length brown hair, amazing cleavage, and an adorable face. But as I shook her hand I couldn't help but stare at the stranger standing before me.

I think it would be fair for me to explain at this point that when I'm in "make out mode" I'm not at all that picky. All I ask is that you're mildly attractive and of legal age, but when you outright misrepresent yourself to someone you agree to swap spit with, it's definite grounds for a bit of shock and awe.

I actually prefer the girls I make out with to have a little meat on them. I've always said, skinny girls make great clothes hangers but when you're in bed I want a woman to look like a woman, not a 12 year old boy...but when the door opens and the girl presenting herself in front of you is literally one hundred pounds more than what her pictures would have you believe, to say that I was taken aback would be putting it nicely. And then there was the issue with the hair. What was once long and healthy was now chopped two inches from her head and replaced with a sickly mini orange afro. A victim of undeveloped grocery store bleach.

She must have noticed the distinct three second pause before I said, "Oooh, ahhh...hey, what's up?"

"Hey you," she said with a smile and a quick hug. "Follow me, we have to take the elevator up to the 7th floor."

I paused before I took that first step; I remember that clearly. It was my conscious saying, "Dude, I think this may be a bad sign. Abort the mission. Abort. Abort."

But I couldn't, she started off towards the elevator and my legs followed suit. I walked awkwardly as if my legs knew better but my feet were running the show. See, I had already committed to the situation by saying, "Yes, yes we WILL make out." Not, "Sure, if we have chemistry." Or, "Let's see how the night goes." Because in all of my juvenile impatience, I simply blurted out, "Yeah sure, why not?"

Those words were ringing in my ears as I tried to think of a quick excuse that wouldn't sound like a quick excuse. In retrospect, any number of excuses would have worked, "I got a call from my ex on the way here and it messed me up," "I ate something bad right before and I think I might need some Pepto," "I have to leave soon to help my friend deal with a break up but I didn't want to ditch out on you," any of these would have gone over well enough. Or at least well enough to make her understand that it wasn't going to happen. But I couldn't do it; I couldn't hurt this nice girl's feelings. I mean, she did invite me over, and she did somehow think I was attractive enough to make out with, and I suppose that is reason enough. I thought, maybe if I just walk in her apartment and play disinterested she might get the hint, as long as I make sure there's not a lull in the conversation for her to make a move I figure I could burn a good half hour of time and sneak out without having to do the deed.

"This is my apartment," she said as she fumbled with her keys to unlock the door. "It's kinda small."

As the door opened, I was met with the pungent stench of cat piss. "Ah," I said squinting my eyes and turning my head to one side. "You have cats?"

"Yeah, how did you know?" She stopped and looked at me.

"Oh," I looked at the floor and off to the left I saw a litter box. "The litter box."

I closed the door behind me and looked around. The apartment looked as if a group of homeless crackheads had been squatting in this small room for months. The overhead exposed lighting illuminated the revolting floors. From wall to wall, and covering almost every inch of flat surface, was the debris of many college keggers; beer bottles, overflowing ash trays teeming with butts and ash spilling to the floor, greasy pizza boxes with discarded pieces of pepperoni and crusts lying along side, an uncovered litter box with hundreds of dry brown and grey turds on the surrounding floor, dishes piled up along the sink counter complete with molding food, brown and rotting along the edges. I've never been known as keeping the cleanest apartment but this was pure squalor. To live and sleep in this 200 square-foot studio apartment would be the equivalent of cohabiting with a den of city sewer rats on a coke binge.

Mortified that anyone could possibly allow a guest into this filth, I cleared a small path to the open futon that served as her bed and only semi-clean place to sit and I took a seat at the end.

"Oh wow," I motioned over to the three-foot glass monstrosity on display in the center of the room. "Whose bong?"

"Ah, that's my roommate's." Was she really expecting me to believe that two people could ever occupy this tiny sewer?

I focused my attention to the table in front of me. Pipes and old bags of weed filled with seeds and stems littered the table. "So, what were you up to tonight?" I asked, trying to buy some time while I formulated an escape route.

"Sitting around, watching 'Everybody Loves Raymond'." I turned my head to the 1970s era console television located an uncomfortable four feet in front of us. Through the black and white haze of the bad reception I could make out the familiar show.

"No cable?" I ask.

"Nah, but if you mess around with the antenna it usually comes in better." -By antenna I believe she was referring to the bent coat hanger forced into the back of the television.

Holy shit, what did I get myself into? I think to myself. I wasn't prepared for this. I mean, I'm no prize by any stretch, and my apartment could use some fixing and cleaning but this may seriously require a call to the health department.

Then I made the grave mistake. I stopped talking. I couldn't think of anything at all to say, I drew a blank. I sat there with my elbow on my knees looking at the garbage underneath my shoes and I was speechless. I felt the silence. Quick, say something, ANYTHING. But it was as if my tongue had jumped ship and was waving back with an evil grin and a middle finger. Dude, you're choking...we've been quiet for too long...I felt each of the five seconds pass slowly like an oncoming car crash I couldn't avoid, I knew it was coming, I could feel it, "So…" she said. I squeezed my eyes closed, trying to steady my nerves. "You wanna make out?"

I turned my neck and cracked it giving me a couple of

seconds to formulate a sentence. Shit, what do I say? This girl is looking at me like she wants to eat me alive, what do I say?

I hung my head in defeat. I knew it was too late once I typed the words "yeah sure." The problem was that I committed to the task and now I was being asked to follow through. I felt her looking at the back of my head waiting for an answer. Eyes still closed I said, "Um, sure."

Sitting to my right she leaned over and put her lips to mine. I sat to her left, sighed and said to myself, ok Chris, if you're going to do this, do it right; make out with her like you've never made out with anyone before. Give her something to tell her friends about. So I did my best.

I wrapped my arms around her, grabbed the back of her head and kissed her with all the intensity I could muster. I positioned my body to face her, pulled my t-shirt over and off my head and climbed on top of her. Commit Chris, commit.

Now, personally, I'm not too much of a fan of kissing and most people understand that when you speak of a make out date, its generally because no one wants to be so brash to say, "Hey, you wanna mess around and possibly have sex?" I'm stuck at this point, but I figure I have three options. First, I suppose can stop. But how awkward would that be? I have nothing in common with this girl and the idea of sitting here amidst the filth and turds all while doing my best at making small talk makes me want to tear out my eyeballs. My second option would be to continue kissing this girl whose mouth is too small for her face, that on top of the fact that I hate kissing for any extended period of time, doesn't sound like a good idea either. Well then what? Well, I suppose there is always the third option, that option being; taking it to the next level.

I recall the cleavage that I saw from her pictures and think it would be fair to at least "see" the boobs at this point. I mean, after all, that is what sold me. I begin kissing her neck and slowly working down to her shirt.

She's wearing a low-cut, yellow top meant to show off

her assets. I could either take her top off (but who knows what surprises lie under that one) or I could do the 8th grade "pull the shirt down and pop the titties out the top" move. Adding to the ridiculousness of the situation, I chose the latter.

I begin the downward descent and kiss on her breasts but I'm all too aware that it's only a matter of time before I'm again bored with this display of middle school sexuality. I begin to laugh in my head. This has all the grace of an "under the bleachers" make out session and I find myself looking to the hazy television to keep myself entertained.

Frustration is building. Literally. In my jeans my friends refer to as my "grape smugglers" because of how they accentuate my 'fruit', my bulge is making attempts at bursting at the seams and a part of me is now exposed and peeking its way out of the top of my low rise women's jeans. I have to let it out but what graceful way is there? Do I say, "Excuse me while I take out my penis because it's beginning to cause pain in my lower abdomen"? And while we're on the subject, if it's coming out, someone is going to have to pay attention to it, even if that someone is me, because I'm definitely not above taking care of myself in times of desperation.

I stop kissing her, lean back on my knees and give her "the look." The "ok, where's this all going" look. Lying on her back and propping herself up on her elbows, she stares at me like a deer in headlights.

We are at what seems to be a stalemate.

I think to myself, Ok. You don't know me; I'll outright say it. Still nothing. She's going to make me say it, isn't she?

An eternity passes and I can't believe I'm a grown ass man in this situation. Fuck it. I'm saying it.

A childish, evil grin washes across my face, I tilt my head down and look up at her and quietly I utter what may be the most embarrassing phase I've ever said, "Psst, hey...I want you to put it in your mouth."

There you go. While it wasn't the most classy or slick

way of going about it, at least it was out there on the table for her to accept or reject as she saw fit.

I leaned back even further waiting her response. Nothing. Deer in headlights. She just keeps staring at me.

Say something damn you. Nod your head yes, scream, "Fuck off!" Just do SOMETHING.

I purse my lips and squint my eyes and think, ok, maybe she didn't hear me, so I'm just gonna say it again. "Hey," I can't keep a straight face anymore and I begin to break character. "You should put it in your mouth." Still, deer in headlights.

I'm a big boy; yes, no, fuck you, wrinkle your nose, whatever just give me something to go on here.

Ok fine. I let out a deep sigh and say fuck it, I'm gonna be a creep and just pull it out and see what happens. Because shit, why not? She can always just tell me to get the fuck out, or call me a freak, but I'll never know until I do it. I give her one last eyebrows-raised look warning, ok woman, that's it...here goes. I look back to her eyes staring at me blankly. But at this point, I simply want to see if I have the guts to brazenly pull out my penis and let it flop in the wind.

I reach down and grab my top button and pause as if to say, listen you, say something or I'm busting this bad boy out. Nothing.

"Ok", my left hand pulls down the top button, my zipper quickly unzips and my erect penis springs out at attention. I am unleashed. The immediate relief in my lower stomach is quickly replaced with the dread feeling of shame because it becomes all to clear that I am a grown man, on a futon, in a room with every light blaring on my shaved crotch, and my fully erect penis is pointing at some random girl whose name I have already forgotten, and we are both staring at one another like the two gangs in Michael Jackson's "Beat It" video.

The seconds slowly tick by and I begin to feel a slight twinge of embarrassment. She clearly doesn't want to come near me. Am I gross? Do I smell? Is my penis horribly disfigured?

Have I simply managed to coerce a handful of naive girls into knocking it around to make me happy while they were holding back vomit? SAY SOMETHING! I scream in my head.

Slowly, ever so slowly, she clumsily pushes off of her elbows like a 90 year-old man getting out of an easy chair. Slowly and awkwardly she eases her way closer to the embarrassment that is protruding out of the top of my undone jeans. Her wheezing becomes more audible as her eyes squint and scrutinize. It's like she's mesmerized. She doesn't look at me; she looks only at IT, as if she has discovered her first penis. I pause, and think to myself that if I move it's going to scare her away like a feral kitten, so I hold my breath and wait.

She continues to stare, now her head is turned to the left in curiosity, and her eyes are still squinting with all the concentration of Bobby Fisher.

Still leaning back on my knees I look for cameras possibly hidden around the well-lit sty. Just as I let out a sigh of ridiculousness and go to shove IT back in my pants, there is movement.

I saw it out of the corner of my eye. Cautiously, like E.T. coming out of the closet for Reeses Pieces, she reaches for it. I hold still. With her right hand she takes a hold of it as if she's investigating a crime scene. She lifts IT and lowers IT, studying each side before I begin to feel an uncoordinated shoving and tugging motion. Awesome, back in the game.

What I've come to learn over the years is that the more positive feedback you give to your partner, the more effort they seem to put in. Putting this theory into practice, you would have thought I was getting a massage by five naked porn stars from the sounds that were coming from me. "Oooh, wow." "Holy shit." "You're amazing."

My inner monologue was in overdrive. For every, "Oooh yesss," I uttered, the aside I whispered to the audience translated to, dude, is this actually happening?

As the yanking continued she did something that took

everyone by surprise. She put it on her lips. Now, one might construe this as a "blow job" but my criteria clearly states that at least 5% of the actual penis must penetrate the mouth and unfortunately for me, it did not. But we were making progress.

"Oooh yeah, just like that." I whispered in the total creepy, sleazy, porn-guy voice. "Uuuh."

Then I heard it again, the wheezing, now even more audible due to the fact she was breathing through her mouth. Under any other circumstances I might think of this as a "next level" technique but due to the angle and her lack of maneuverability I took this as an early sign of an asthma attack. Quickly, I leap off the futon and stand; she sits up and moves herself to the edge for a better angle.

"Ok, NOW it's on," I say to the imaginary audience in my head.

Much to my dismay, more of the same. Here I am, standing here glowing in the bright light of the shade-less lamp as some girl does "the tummy monster" on my ever-deflating penis. Just I lace my fingers behind my neck and look toward the ceiling, she stops and for the first time looks at me.

Did I do something wrong, I think. Can she hear the laughing voices in my head? Oh, shit, I'm caught. I look at her with raised eyebrows, smile an uncomfortable toothy grin and I shrug one shoulder.

"Um..." she says.

Pause.

"Um..."

Oh god no.

"I want you..."

Don't say it. Don't you say it. Don't you say it.

"To put it...inside me."

AAAAHHHHH! The audience yells.

My eyes bug out and I breathe in deep. Don't yell. Don't yell. Holy shit, Chris...how do you get out of this one? This never would have happened if you hadn't agreed to it in the first place you sucker. How do you get out of this one? Abort. Abort. Abor...

Wait, I think to myself. You wanted the filth and now you got it and you're turning yellow and running. Jump in. Do it. Why not?

"Uh...um...well, ok," I say as she hands me a yellow condom. "Take off your pants."

With all the dexterity of a kindergartner, I scramble to shove the condom on my semi-erect penis. I look over and see her naked from the waist down, still wearing the low-cut, yellow shirt, lying back waiting for me. I assume the position, give a sigh, a pause, and a "if you're going to do this, do it right" pep talk to myself and begin the task.

Spitting in my hand, I reach in-between her legs to make sure everything is right where it should be, lubricate what needs to be lubricated and slowly embark on my journey. Remember Chris, if you're gonna do this...make her remember it, I say. Not too fast right off the bat, you don't want to come off as some eager teenager. Show some style and skill. Do your slow and subtle moves.

I'm on my knees and she's lying on her back, one foot above the ground on the old and bent-in-the-middle futon. Ok, ok...not bad. You're doing just fine, Chris. You ready to kick it into second gear? I say to myself. Ok, let's do this.

I lurch forward and my face is in hers, we kiss and I remember why I stopped kissing her, so I turn my head to my right and rest it on her shoulder. I begin thrusting faster and harder. As I take my hand and position it on my shoulder for leverage, I get hit in the face with the pungent stench of a three-day-old dead animal. "Aaaccch," I choke out, and I smell my hand. The hand that was just previously used for lubrication. But how? She had just taken a shower and her hair is still wet.

I quickly turn my head to my left. I'm thrusting and I'm concentrating. Please let me finish this as soon as possible. I thought I was ready for this level of filth. I'm not. Clearly, I am not.

I make promises to the pervert internet gods that in the future I won't bite off more than I can chew.

Eyes closed tight I'm thinking of super models and naked girls from the internet. Beads of concentration sweat form on my brow and I wipe them away. Concentrate. Finish. Finish. Finis...Wait...what the?

What's that noise? I hear scratching. It's close.

Scratch. Scratch. Scratch.

What the..? My brow furrows and I frantically search the room for the only thing that's standing between me finishing and me leaving.

Scratch. Scratch.

AAAHH! WHAT THE FUC...

I prop myself up on my hands and extend my arms and I look directly to my left and I see it.

My head is a foot and a half away from the litter box. The scratching is coming from the cat. The scratching is coming from the paw trying to cover the fresh brown and hot TURD he had just expended.

HOLY! FUCKING! SHIT! GET! ME! OUT! OF! HERE! My inner monologue screams.

Ok ok ok, Chris. Finish this NOW. Let's kick it into overdrive...and here we go. Concentrate. Concentrate.

To the right: dead animal. To the left: cat shit.

I push myself back up and on to my knees and I begin banging this girl with every muscle in my back like only a madman with a purpose could. I'm banging and banging. I lift her legs for support and all I can think of is how it feels like I'm bro-hugging two full-grown dudes. I hold on to her legs for dear life and I bang like there's a million dollars waiting to come out of my penis and all I have to do is work for it just a little harder.

Sweat dripping from my face, neck and chest. "I'm gonna...I'm gonna..." I say to her.

"On my tits," she says. I spring to my feet and being

careful to avoid stepping in the cat shit, I stand next to her. I reach down to pull off the condom and it's red. Red and dripping with BLOOD! "OOO OOH GOO OOOD." I scream as my body simultaneously convulses in horror and orgasm.

I frantically yank at the condom and it stretches and comes off with a good "thwack". Disgusted and sweaty and ejaculating I throw the bloody condom to the floor and it lands directly alongside the poop that could no longer fit inside the actual litter box. "Hooooly shiiiiiit!" I yell to the ceiling.

Panting and sweating, with bloody penis in hand, I look to the cat shit on the floor and say, "I have to go to the bathroom."

Without hesitation I scramble my way to the bathroom through the greasy pizza boxes, dirty underwear, and dented beer cans. I rush in and slam the door behind me. Immediately I begin ferociously washing my hands with a bar of green soap. Wash. Rinse. Repeat.

I dry my hands, rest them on the edge of the sink, look in the mirror, and say quietly to myself, "What hell did you just do?"

I breathe out for what seems like the first time since I walked in and I shake my head back and forth. Ok dude, just pee and get dressed and leave this haunted house as quickly as possible.

I slowly lift the toilet seat with my foot and as I do so, I notice the underside of the seat is brown. -Not just a spot or two like in a truck stop bathroom, but like someone had purposely lifted the seat and treated that toilet to the meanest and most violent watery shart known to man. I recoil in repugnance and put my hands to my face. No. No. No. Just get me out. Get me out!

I walk out of the bathroom and she's sitting on the futon, still in the low-cut yellow shirt yet naked from the waist down . I grab my clothes and start putting my right leg in my jeans. "So, I guess that was better than watching 'Everybody Loves

Raymond'," I say with a coy smile and a jerk of the shoulders.

"Uh. Yeah," she blurts out, continuing to not look at me.

"Um, oooookay...I'm gonna get going."

"Oh, huh, so you're just gonna leave now," she asks while turning to face me, staring daggers into my chest.

Timidly, I pick at the doorframe, "Well, I mean...I thought that's why I was here? To make out, right?" I ask.

"Well, you can find your way to the elevator," she responds, curtly.

Bewildered and zombie-like, I walked out on to the sidewalk and hailed a cab.

"I did something bad."

"Christopher, what did you do?" Gheesling yells.

"It was...vile."

"I don't understand." Confused, she asked, "But why did you do it?"

"Because I committed to the task."

Make Your Mark

ഇറ

Humbling wouldn't even begin to describe it.

Hunched over, elbows out, pedaling down Milwaukee Avenue with the pulsating early morning sun already burning my face into a dripping mess, I said over and over, "There's got to be a better way." Third time must have been the charm because the right cuff of my jeans got caught between the crank and the bike chain.

"Oh seriously? Fuck you," I yelled, coasting to the curb.

A few months prior I got the great idea to move from the comfort of the suburbs to the heart of dirty Chicago to wait tables for pretentious gay men and to begin the journey of my cosmetology education.

"Beauty school" is a hellacious process comprised of droning eight hour days where one spends hours at a time practicing their hair rolling skills on the off chance an army of senior citizens walk through the door and demand a roller set in thirty minutes or less. Endless hours of practice and repeat. For eight hours, five days a week.

Eight hours, five days a week doesn't allow for much of a social life let alone a full time job. But since the city of Chicago isn't giving away free or reduced rent to anyone possessing the ability to make a perfect finger wave, I spent my nights immediately following school serving moderately priced pasta dishes to the finest of Lakeview's gay population.

I would be the last server allowed to pick a serving section due to the fact that I was the last person to arrive because I was the only grown adult who worked there while still in school full time. As I washed the glossy remnants of brown hair gel from in-between my fingers, my manager would approach and say, "Since you were the last one to arrive, you know you have to stay until close again, right?"

This became standard. I would close out the restaurant, stacking chairs and wiping down salt and peppershakers until the lights went out. If I was lucky, I would fall into bed around 1:00 a.m.

My alarm would begin its screaming assault at 6 a.m. in order for me to make the 8:00 a.m. train to school, or as the kids in beauty school would affectionately refer to it, the "piss trolley." The purple line EL train heading north at 8 a.m. was filled with young beauty school students carrying mannequin heads with partially rolled hair rods as homework. The arrival of the sun let the city's homeless who reside in the EL cars know to wake up and begin the day. Most of them also made sure to relieve themselves in the corner of the car, which always made for a nice eye-opening early morning aroma as we dodged the rivulets of yellow urine at our feet.

Trudging through the brutal two seasons of Chicago – burning and freezing – this became my life for an entire year.

During that year, the restaurant I worked at went through some changes. In order to meet increasing demand, they opened seven new restaurants to alleviate the congestion at our location. But congestion is what paid my bills. So after a couple of months, my weekly income dropped to roughly $200 a week and despite living in one of the most affordable apartments in Lakeview, my rent might as well have been a million dollars because I couldn't find the means to pay for that, bills, and food.

This resulted in PB&Js.

Peanut butter and jelly became my staple food source. I would eat four sandwiches a day; two at lunch, and two as I walked in the door returning from school. That, coupled along with whatever food I could steal off customers' plates, compromised my diet for almost an entire year. Only in retrospect can I see the affect the lack of vitamins had on my skin, sleep and overall demeanor.

During our lunch breaks at school some of the girls would ask me, "Oh no you ain't eatin' another peanut butter and jelly sandwich, you broke ass motherfucka."

"Man, my ass is broke," I would say back in my best Chris Rock impersonation.

"Motherfucka, you best get yo ass a purple Visa"

"What's a purple Visa?"

The girls at the table found my naiveté amusing. They went on to tell me that the "purple Visa," as it's known in certain urban circles, is properly referred to by the city of Chicago as the LINK card. Replacing physical food stamps, the LINK card resembles a purple credit card; the recipient is given a certain amount of money for food determined by the board of welfare and can use the card at participating grocery stores.

"So it's a welfare card?"

"Yeah."

"Do you have one?" I asked, cringing in fear of offending.

"Shiiit," they said in chorus as they each pulled out a purple card and slapped it on the lunch table.

"Motherfucka, it's free money. You better get yo ass on it."

I spent the rest of my lunch that day with my head on the table feigning sleep as I talked it over in my mind. Could I go on "welfare?" I mean, I would be "one of those" people. I don't want to have to tell my children one day that "daddy was on welfare when he was in beauty school."

That night on the train ride home I called my notoriously levelheaded friend Dennis to ask his advice.

"Ok, let me ask you a question," he said.

"Are you hungry?"

"If you mean, 'am I sick of eating peanut butter and jelly for two meals a fucking day?' then yes."

"Do you have enough money to pay your bills?"

"Dude, I'm stealing cable, what do you think?"

"Do you make less than the poverty level?"

"If I'm lucky I'm making $800 a month. That's not even ten grand a year. So I would say yes."

At the end of a long pause he said, "So get your ass down to the welfare office and apply."

The thought of going to a "welfare office" terrified me. What if someone I grew up with saw me and went home and told everyone I knew? "Man, that Christopher is doing terrible. I saw him walking into the welfare office with dark circles under his eyes and I think I saw a bit of peanut butter and jelly on the corner of his mouth."

"No. I won't do it," I said as I walked through the door of my apartment.

I opened the cupboard to grab my loaf of white bread, untwisted the bag and saw that only the two moldy ends remained. Furious, I threw the bag into the sink, grabbed my bike, rode over to Dennis', walked through the door and asked, "Where's your computer? I need to know what forms I have to fill out."

The following Monday I found myself rolling down Lincoln Avenue with a messenger bag slung over my shoulder filled with three forms of identification to prove I was a citizen, a copy of my lease and piles of over-due bills. Crossing the intersection of Milwaukee and Fullerton I felt the sweat beads forming on my back, causing my shirt to stick tight to me.

"There has got to be a better way."

Locking my bike in front of the dismal gray building, I looked up at the sign that read "Illinois State Welfare Department," sighed, hung my head and said, "Ok, let's get this over with."

I opened the door and was met by an enormous security guard who inspected my bag and gave me a quick pat down. I thought this a bit odd as I walked up the stairs to the third floor. I reached the top of the stairs and pushed through the glass door and was immediately stopped again by another large security guard seated near the entrance.

"Can I help you?" he said, standing up.

"Yeah, I believe I have an appointment."

"Can I see yo' ID?" he asked in a tone of disbelief, as if I was trying to sneak backstage at a Motley Crüe concert.

"Christopher Gutierrez."

Looking at a clipboard he said, "You have an appointment with one of the counselors at 11:00 a.m. They will call your name. Go sit down." He pointed in the direction of the end of the short hall.

I put my license back into my wallet, turned around, and began my walk down the hallway. As I rounded the corner to the waiting room it was just as I had suspected. Brown plastic chairs were haphazardly strewn throughout the yellowing room. It was as if a decorator from 1960s East Berlin came in with a paint roller of bleak and went to town, and leaving the job unfinished.

I took a seat as far away from anyone as possible so I could read my book in peace. But I couldn't take my eyes off of the aesthetics. Paneling torn from the sides of the walls by hordes of lunatic children. Yellow and brown spots molding in the back corners, leading me to believe that this is where the nighttime residents of the purple line came to spend their daylight hours. Groups of families are scattered around the lifeless and dimly lit industrial room. I re-adjust in my chair and my foot kicks apart a half-eaten hamburger. I look at the floor beneath it and I can see the hard yellow tiles chipping at the corners.

"There has got to be a better way," I say under my breath.

I look to the counter where the over worked and sad employees maintain their sanity. They look broken and used up, as if they throw their hands up every morning and say, "This is what my life is to become."

But then my eyes focus on the people waiting in the seats and my heart builds with empathy. In front of me is a mother holding onto what looks like a garbage bag of her clothes. She doesn't look crazy or homeless, she simply looks like life had dealt her a rotten hand.

"Jennifer, can you please just sit still for a minute," she says to her daughter, trying to keep voice low.

A pretty young blonde girl sits next to the garbage bag and pulls out a blonde doll that resembles herself. But this doll is dirty and naked and its hair is falling out. Jennifer plays with it on her knees, making it dance to the left and the right, and she sings a song I don't recognize. Her mother sits still and quiet with her eyes focused on the dirty white wall in front of her, her arm around the bag as if it's all she has.

An old man in a brown cardigan slowly walks in with a cane. He looks about 80, with thin gray hair and thick glasses tied around the back of his head. He searches for a spot to sit and carefully maneuvers into the chair.

A mother of five children sits across from me. She sits knitting what looks like it will be a winter hat while her five children cause chaos through the room, taking the pens from the counter to draw pictures of trees and suns and children on the walls. It all just blends together with the dirt so no one says much.

Growing up in the middle class suburbs, I had the impression that people on welfare were "taking advantage of the system" and were to blame for high taxes. That "these people just need to pick themselves up by the bootstraps and make something of their lives." Today I felt ashamed. How could I have ever sat and pontificated over a hot meal with hot and cold running water and a warm bed at home and had the audacity to make judgments about the lives of others? How could I have possibly known about the mothers that were beaten and thrown out by their bread-winning husbands and left to fend for themselves on the streets of the city?

How could I have the arrogance to condemn a system while children who now stand before me beg their mothers for the McDonalds that mockingly stands across the street? It's not because they're spoiled kids who want their way, but because they are hungry. Because they want what all the rest of the kids their age have and that mommy can't buy because she's desperately trying to keep the landlord from serving them eviction notices.

While I'm certain there are cases of abuse within this system, I shake and hang my head knowing that there are children sharing space with me in this very room who will go to bed with their stomachs tied up in knots and will wake up and wear the same clothes to school that they did they day before.

Jennifer looks at me over two rows of brown chairs and smiles and holds up her doll to show me.

I look her in the eyes and smile and while I'm tempted to, I don't look away.

I hold my gaze and think about how Jennifer doesn't know the pain yet; living in poverty is all she knows. She doesn't know that her doll is outdated and ugly. She sees the beauty where no one else does. She's perfectly happy and content and smiling...all within the yellowing walls of a welfare office. She's going to be stunning one day, but all I can see is the life that is ahead of her and a chill runs to my fingers knowing the odds that the ugliness of life and the struggle of her mother's journey will turn this adorable little princess into a hardened and jaded woman.

I hold my gaze because I have a feeling Jennifer won't remember this moment.

But I will.

I sit humbled and embarrassed that I'm even here. That I have the audacity to ask for money while I have a roof, peanut butter and jellys and no need to keep my belongings in a plastic bag.

I close my book and just as i reach down for my things to leave a gruff and smoky voice yells, "Christopher Gutierrez!"

I stand and walk to the teller window.

"Hi, I'm Christopher Gutierrez. I believe I have an appointment."

"Yeah. Walk through that door and your assigned counselor will be with you in a moment" she says, pointing to the door on her right.

I walk through and am greeted by a middle-aged man who is holding so much paperwork he doesn't even look at me when he shakes my hand.

"Mr. Gutierrez, take a seat. So why are you here?"

I sit down across from him in his cubicle.

"Um, well. I don't make much money and I'm in school forty hours a week and I'm working forty hours a week. I just need to make the ends meet."

"Did you bring all the necessary forms of identification?"

"Yes sir."

"Ok, give me everything you have and fill out these forms. If everything you say checks out we will see what we can do for you." He takes the papers from my hands, doesn't look at me and walks away.

I begin to fill out the pages of questions.

Everything from "How many people do you live with?" to "Are you sending money home to another country?"

At the very end of the document there is a line that says, "I attest that all the information is true to my knowledge."

And below it is a line that reads: Sign here or make your mark.

Make your mark.

That's what stood out most to me that day. Not the sweaty bike ride, not the pride swallowing two hour wait, not even Jennifer in her pretty pink and white flowered dress.

"Make your mark" was just an indicative of the situation. That there was someone without the knowledge of something as simple as signing their name that would have warranted the writers of the contract to say "Yeah, we better put that 'make your mark' clause in there." That someone with such a lack of basic skills lives in my city and is expected to "make a living." What jobs could they possibly get if they can't do something as simple as signing their name? And what job of that kind would help support a wife and children?

I paused with the pen in my hand over the line. I couldn't help but be taken aback by this. My counselor walked into the cubicle behind me.

"Ok, Mr. Gutierrez. You are approved for $150 in groceries a month."

Despite my paltry victory, I stared at the floor. I just couldn't get past the fact that there were so many people struggling to simply live a meager existence in this world. A world where simple survival is good enough. Odds were Jennifier's mother would never know what it felt like to live her dream or to have unlimited opportunities presented before her. The people that sat in those brown chairs were there sacrificing their dignity for food. They simply wanted to eat. They sat in those chairs heartsick and humbled and after they "made their mark" they would walk out that door and return to a world that would only speak of them in whispers and in shame.

That day, I walked out of that office with the clarity of a new beginning. I promised myself I would give the life that pulsated through my veins a fighting chance to make those that loved me proud and that I wouldn't waste a breath of air or take for granted the generosity of my friends because it would be a slap in the face to everyone who sat with me in that office.

I pedaled home hard that day. Motivated by those faces, I was determined to make my mother smile when she spoke my name. Or at least to go down swinging as I pushed out my last breath. Jennifier, the old man, my counselor. I swore that I would never see them again. And I swore to live my life with open eyes and an open heart because the world doesn't need another callous asshole who points a finger at everyone else while squandering away the fortune and the freedom and the five senses he or she has been given.

I pedaled hard because I learned how to live that day.

The Inherent Power of Cheesecake

෨෬

I took each stair fast, as if I could convince my racing heart that I wasn't nervous. Each step was conscious and solid and intentional. My legs pushed my body up the old wooden stairs to the second floor landing and my fingers tingled in anticipation but I would be damned if I would give her the satisfaction of knowing she had me like that. Because she had me like that.

I rushed up the last flight of stairs, open bottle of coke in one hand and a bag containing cheesecake and DVDs in the other. Before I took the last four steps to the third floor landing, she opened the door. With four steps left I saw her for the first time. The first time in real life. My throat immediately made note of the fact that she was stunning and it began to make breathing difficult and short. My inexperienced heart panicked as it was thrown to the lions and my eyes glazed over in anticipation...but my face knew better, it understood that I reeked of fear and my lack of sophistication was now at the helm. But my well-trained arsenal of words was prepared for such an occasion and luckily they came through with impeccable timing and surprising accuracy.

"Hey."

"Hey."

My First Hero

ഔരു

The nausea came at once. There was no warning.

It was ten at night as she attempted to back the car out of our driveway to go work her second job, I pressed my open hands and hot face against the cold window while kneeling in the orange and brown chair and cried. It wasn't the kind of crying I was familiar with. They weren't the crocodile tears of a child who didn't get his way, or the welling up from seeing blood coming from your knee after a bike accident.

This was different.

This was the deep down gut-wrenching heaving sobbing that came from the depths of your stomach and left your back muscles sore the next day. The kind that kicked your glands into overdrive and left the whites of your eyes bloodshot red the next morning. The kind of crying that made your knees weak, walking difficult, and your hands tremble. It was the kind of wailing that is left for parents who outlive their children. It was the kind of crying that children shouldn't know about. It was the kind of crying that I learned about that winter.

The year before, my brother and grandfather had been in a heart-wrenching, torn-from-the-headlines accident. My grandfather was attempting to cross the street while holding the hand of his two year-old grandson and they were struck by a car. This resulted in extreme trauma, comas, and within the week, two deaths. One week my grandpa was making my brother and I

147

eat gross oatmeal, the next he was lying in a coffin smelling of the cover up and foundation powder used to mask the injuries he had suffered to his face. My brother's funeral was a few days later.

These events threw a monkey wrench to the already shaky machine that was my family.

My mother was a textbook caregiver: cooking, cleaning, and working two jobs. I have never seen her sit still or have a moment of peace to herself. She was always a bit high strung, tired, and overworked. Since my mother was sixteen she has had to support a family. She was left to care for her little sister after my grandmother died of a heart attack at the age of forty-four, eventually she and my father produced me out of wedlock. Never has she lived a day of her life selfishly. She was just the right opportunity for my father to exploit.

My father was born in the hard streets of Chicago. In gangs throughout his adolescence, he called juvenile correctional facilities home off and on from the age of twelve to eighteen for everything from arson to auto theft, eventually earning himself the nickname Cadillac Charlie. He was loud and brash, and his breath always smelled of alcohol, even in the morning. He smiled more than he yelled, and was always ready with a new racist joke, yet he loved Motown and Richard Pryor more than anyone I have ever known.

Somehow during the seventies he managed to pull himself out of the mayhem and addictions that had enveloped his life to become a paramedic and ambulance driver and fool everyone, including himself, that he was a respectable and productive member of society; this was how he met my mother.

My mother was working as a nurse at a hospital where my father would transport patients; it was here that he managed to charm her into a date and eventually a pregnancy. I was born into the hands of my mother's co-workers, not much long after.

My unwed parents moved us out to the suburbs two years later to give me a better life. To give me a yard, a chance, and decent public schooling. For a few years, everything seemed to be going fairly well, that was until my father's drinking, drugs, and womanizing began to rear their ugly heads once again; just in time for the accident.

The accident was the bowling ball and we were the pins; each of us went flying into different directions. My mother lost her son and her father, my father lost his son, and I lost everyone. Half of my family was dead, and what remained was a father who, despite all the progress of the years prior, couldn't fight his genetic design and dove head first into the addiction his father and his father before him had passed down through one simple shot of semen. So while my mother surrounded herself with good friends and work, my father was off for days at a time on cocaine and hooker binges. Countless nights I was left alone to sleep in the silent dark of my house, or to be awoken in the middle of the night by my drunken father. Somewhere in the next year he managed to give my mother a daughter; a daughter he fought to name Erika. -My dead brothers name was Eric.

It took years for my passive mother to work up the strength to throw my father out. I gave her my blessing. Now it was just us. In a matter of just a couple of years, my family went through a hostile takeover and I was left in a position I was not qualified for: Man of the House.

The weight and pressure to help maintain a house, baby-sit, and order my own food while my mom was working one of her two jobs was overwhelming. I was responsible for going to bed at a reasonable hour in a dark and lonely house, waking myself up for school the next morning, and trying and do my best to somehow find my way in the unforgiving world of elementary school. In addition to all of this, I was a kid who had recently lost most of his family.

I didn't understand my role. The confusion tore at my brain, and at night, the tears would choke me to sleep and I would pray to God to keep my mother safe.

All I ever wanted was my mother to stay alive. To keep

149

breathing and driving and laughing and caring.

I put all my eggs in one basket. Whether she knew it or not, she held my faith and belief in all that was good in her hands because she was the only true representation of honesty, goodness, and sincerity I had ever known.

She was fair, even when she punished me. She loved me, even and especially when I made it nearly impossible. She sacrificed her happiness so that my sister and I would not have to endure a life of poverty, as she did when she was young.

My nights were punctuated with the fear that if I woke up and didn't pray to God to keep her safe before I fell back asleep, she would be the victim of a terrible car accident, or she would be robbed or kidnapped and I would be to blame because I knew God wanted me to ask to keep her safe and if for some reason she left this planet, I knew it would be my fault for missing the opportunity to keep her guarded and preserved and away from harm.

I prayed seven times a day because I thought that seven was a "holy" number. I prayed seven times because six was evil and eight was my favorite number and if I prayed eight times God would know that it was my favorite number and that would be seen as selfish.

So seven times a day, usually before bed, I would say the Lord's Prayer and follow it with, "And God bless Mommy and keep her safe from all evil and harm and please watch over her." I would then say please three times afterward to a fade out.

PLEASE.

Please.

Pleeeeease.

I would clutch my hands so tightly together that I could see the white in my knuckles, because if God could see that, He could see how much conviction was in my words, and if He could see that, then maybe He would realize just how serious I was about how much I loved my mother and maybe, just maybe, He would give me one more day with her on this planet. And if I could clench my eyes together hard enough to squeeze tears in the corners of my eyes, God would see that at that second no one loved their mother as much as I loved my mother. If I could make tears roll down my cheek I just knew God would personally keep watch over her.

So, when my mother left the house under any circumstances, I would pray. If she left and people were around I would loosely bring together my right and left hands intertwining at the finger tips and silently mouth the Lord's Prayer and send the desperate words to a God I knew was listening closely for the slightest inkling of insincerity so He could strike down my mommy with cancer...and I would be guilty, and God would punish me for the rest of my days with a long life and an unforgettable and overwhelming guilt that I would never have the ability to pray away.

If I could feel God watching me closely enough I would excuse myself to my room to "grab something I forgot" so I could rush to my bed, lie down, and give the appropriate attention to the words that would keep my mother alive. Alive so she could keep the house, so she could accomplish her goal of going back to school, so she could be my beacon of honor and virtue, and most importantly, to tell me she loved me via phone call and set my heart at ease before I fell asleep that night.

Looking out of the window in that orange chair, I sobbed so hard that I began to heave. With the sleeve of my blue thermal pajamas, I wiped the tears from my neck and the snot from my nose. I saw that my mother couldn't make it through the snow and out of the driveway. Rolling down the window, my mother waved to me to come outside.

Was she going to tell me that she wasn't leaving?

Was this the time she would tell me that I would never have to leave her side?

I ran to the post that held my fuzzy hooded winter coat, put it on, shoved my little feet in my moon boots and ran outside.

"What did you need?" I asked, panting, out of breath

from running through the snow.

"Can you shovel the snow out from behind me?" She asked.

My bright eyes fell to the snow and I lost all sense of urgency.

My hope vanished and I slowly walked back to the garage and grabbed a snow shovel. I returned and began heaving clumps of fresh and wet snow off of our driveway and into the neighbor's yard.

I worked slowly because the snow was damp and heavy like a giant snow-cone...but really I worked slowly because I knew the moment I let her go in that weather, she would be out of my protected sight and God would take her and end her life. He would kill her because I wasn't a good enough son, because I didn't protect her from the danger. He would see it, and I would pay.

I looked through the rear window and I could see her face illuminated by the dome light above her. She was applying blush. I could see her straining to see her reflection in the small visor vanity mirror. She brushed and waited for me.

I took longer than I should have. I pushed that shovel with a lump in my throat and watery eyes, but I was old enough to know that if I had screamed, "Mom, please don't leave or God will kill you!" She would have chuckled and told me that I was too old to be acting so unreasonable. Like a passenger with a bad feeling before a doomed flight, I breathed in wet and stinging air that got caught in my ribs and made my heart beat through my shirt.

"Are you almost done back there, slow poke?" She said with a smile as she manually rolled down the window of the rusted Datsun 260Z that she was so proud of.

"Yeah."

"Okay, come here and give Mommy a kiss."

I walked to the window and put my right arm around her neck and gave her a kiss on the cheek. I could smell her favorite perfume, Ninja, coming from her neck. It smelled terrible, but it was what I could afford to buy her from the local department stores for every holiday from Easter to Christmas. She wore it every day because I bought it for her, and it made me smile every time I saw her spray it because I saw her smile back at me. I think she knew it made me happy because I couldn't hide my big toothy grin whenever I caught wind of it.

I hugged her longer than normal that night. I'm sure she didn't notice, but I did. I felt safe with the smell of her perfume, the warmth of the dashboard heat, and my arm around her.

"Honey, I have to go." She said breaking our embrace.

"Um, Mom," I said, desperately trying to hide my quivering bottom lip. "Please be careful."

"I'll see you in the morning," she replied. I could see her left arm cranking the window up and hear the grinding of the car's transmission as it shifted into reverse.

The car moved slowly and carefully backward, as I stood in front of it on the driveway that had already been covered in a fresh layer of glistening snow. As she fell away from me, the headlights innocently turned each snowflake into a tiny flicker of light so that the moment seemed surreal.

And the car was moving away from me.

"Mom," I said, while taking a slow step forward.

"God...please...please, don't do this God."

The car backed out on to the street. I heard the grinding noise of first gear, a rev of the engine, and then it moved forward.

"Please..."

As the car gained momentum, I could still see my mother inside glowing underneath the overhead light as she waved goodbye. Everything in my being told me it would be the last time I would see her.

I walked towards the retreating car with the shovel gripped loosely in my right hand, dragging and scraping it along the blacktop of the driveway.

"MOM!" I screamed, "NO!"

Then I ran.

I sprinted behind the car. Blinded by guilt, fear, watery eyes, God's wrath, and the insecurities of a 10 year-old boy. I ran with teeth clenched, jawbones protruding, chin up, and the motivation of saving my mother's life.

I ran and the car got smaller.

I yelled louder.

And the car got smaller.

I screamed for mercy to an unforgiving God.

And the car disappeared into the black and white of a suburban nighttime snowstorm.

I dropped to my knees in the middle of the street, wailing and pounding my gloved fists into the snow as if she was already dead. I was far too old for this behavior, but my lungs and my heart and my eyes and the trembling of my knees knew differently.

I cried for my brother who God took just as he was becoming my best friend.

I cried for my grandfather who was my light, my teacher, mentor, and God incarnate.

And I screamed to the heavens for taking the last shred of substance left in my life. I screamed out love until my voice cracked and my tear ducts pulsated; I screamed for my mother.

I picked myself up out of the snow and began walking home.

I picked up my shovel and walked up the driveway towards the front door of the house, and as I walked I promised myself that despite what plans were in the stars, I would never let God know I loved another living soul.

If those words came out of my mouth, He would know what was most important to me and He would add that name to his ever-amassing arsenal of ways to stab at my heart. And as my boots carried the Titanic of distrust on my shoulders back home that night, I swore I would never let Him touch my heart again.

I was a child, dragging a shovel, burning with hate, under God's mocking winter night. I looked up into the darkness and knew He was watching. I screamed at the pepper sky, "You will not win!"

The next morning I was woken up by the sound of my mother's keys opening the front door. As she walked into the kitchen, I could smell the donuts and coffee she had brought for breakfast. I ran downstairs with the excitement of a child on Christmas morning, and I hugged her around her waist.

"Whoa, well good morning to you too," she said, smiling, trying not to drop the coffee she was holding.

I looked up at her and opened my mouth but nothing came out. I couldn't say it. I wanted to. I wanted her to know how grateful I was that she was in my life. I wanted her to know that my heart did not yet possess the ability to stand on its own. I wanted to tell her how she was my world, my motivation, and my perfection. But while I may have forgotten about the pact I had made the night before with the black sky, my heart and my mouth, driven by self-preservation, had not.

That morning, I sat at our cheap and outdated yellow and white kitchen table and as I shoved donuts into my mouth I thought about how that day was the first day of my life I had not told my mother I loved her when I should have. While my love for her beamed from my eyes, ears, and fingers, I knew that her existence was more important than the trite words of a selfish child.

The next day, when it was bedtime, my mother hugged me and said, "I love you, Chrissy-poo."

I turned my head and gave a simple, "Night, Mom," and walked away.

I walked in my room and laid face down in the bed, crying. I felt like I was betraying the one person left in this world that actually deserved and appreciated my love, the one person who, after losing all that was dear to her in the last year, NEEDED to hear those words.

Each night after that, I could see my mom's face wilt just a bit after my curt dismissal of her words.

Each night after that I would stay up late thinking how I was destroying my resolve and melting away at my very soul by allowing my heart to fall away from my protector and the very star I wished upon.

I knew that telling your mother that you love her shouldn't be difficult, especially if she's not only your hero, but your champion and living reminder of the good that was left in the world. I adored her, but after years of NOT telling her, finding the right words and the right time seemed to be obscured by the damage that time takes on a coward.

Fifteen years later, I drove my car into the city to wish her a happy birthday. I parked and my palms held intermission on the steering wheel. Why was this so difficult? Why was there even a hint of hesitation when all I wanted to do was be completely honest and grant a reprieve to my heart's fifteen-year sentence. I opened the door and stepped out to a blistery and rainy fall evening.

I walked to the wooden steps of her home, my uneasy legs taking one step at a time. I hesitated, took a deep breath and rang her doorbell. She answered like she always did, wearing her mom sweatshirt and a smile, and she gave a great big hug to her undeserving son.

"Well, its about time you got here," she said, taking my coat.

"Happy birthday, Mom," I said, extending a card.

"Oh honey, we'll do gifts after dinner."

"No. Um, Mom. Can you open this one now?"

"Um, okay. Sure." She said.

She opened the card and I watched her eyes read from left to right, starting high then gradually going lower until the smile left her face and I saw the beginnings of tears well in the bottom of her eyes.

She closed the card, looked at it then looked at me.

We were suspended in time.

Slowly, carefully, and deliberately, she smiled the familiar comforting smile I had so desperately craved since the night I had dragged that shovel back up the driveway.

She leaned in and hugged me.

The combination of her arms around my waist while she held the card in her hands and her head on my shoulder released every ounce of hate and distrust I had screamed into that night sky.

She held me and I felt weightless, and she hugged me like she was proud. She hugged me good and strong, like she never wanted to let me go, because she knew it took everything in me to write the words: I LOVE YOU.

She hugged me hard and rocked me back and forth for a long time like I was a child, and I didn't stop her.

Because I didn't want her to stop.

In a whisper she said, "Thank you, honey."

As we rocked back and forth, I cleared the lump from my throat and spoke the words that had been held captive behind clenched teeth for too many years, "I love you, Mom."

I felt her smile grow on my shoulder, "I know, honey. I know."

ABOUT THE AUTHOR:

By day, Christopher Gutierrez works as a hair stylist at a pretentious downtown Chicago salon. By night, he is busy running through the streets in the smallest and most embarrassing running shorts he can find, supporting the local punk rock and hardcore music scenes, playing Dance Dance Revolution on Playstation and eating more Chicago pizza and sushi than anyone should all while finding the time to run his mouth daily on his blog; askheychris.livejournal.com. He travels throughout the United States speaking into microphones to anyone that will listen. He is a grown ass man, he is still straight edge and he resides in Chicago, Illinois. This is his second book.

ALSO BY CHRISTOPHER GUTIERREZ:

On the Upswing of Life, Love and Regret

The Dirt of an Electric Boy (spoken word cd)

৪৩০৪

Without these people this book would not be in your hands and I would not walk this earth.

Peter Rullo, Steven Kane, James Grimes, Nyree Bushnaq, Jordan Lovis, David Cronin, Justin Pence, John Regan, Jay Jancetic, Sara Appino, Jonathan Mckaig, Michael Rankin, Timothy Mailrath, Joseph Principe, Eric Bonny, Robert Richards, Laura Prusik, Nicole Vurusic, Travis McCoy, Disashi Lumumba-Kasongo, Eric Roberts, Luke Gray, Tony Pacenta, Michael Ski, Timothy Biedron, Katherine Sigel, Andrea Tuohy, Rachel Race, Dennis Rittenhouse, David Leist, Jim Sevcik, Eric Bee, Charles Mark, Matthew Gugala, Cassandra Ruhlow, Cassandra Nowicki, Jack Marin, Emily Gillett, Joseph Partyka, Andy Nelson, Peter Grossman, Daniel Polak, Isaac Galatzer-Levy, Daniel Suh, Patrick Stumph, Nicholas Scimeca, Katherine Truscott, Michael Way, Alicia Way, Meghan Sanders, Elissa Ayadi, Sarah Suvan, Eliza Siep, Jeffree Star, Jenna Kimmel, Lindsie Christine, Sara Koeritz, Brittnay Balluff, Rachel Flora, Brooke Bunnell, Fabiola Quinones, Ayala Ofek, Kelly Gheesling, Neeraj Kane, Rachel Johnston, Brooke Matelis, Gianna Nowicki, Heather Ferrari, Matthew Sharp, Steven Riola, Justin Thompson, Kathryn Roach, Amy Roach, Andrea Herzog, Heather Stoffels, Maria Araya, Dina Yousif, Marta Wozniak, Carina Harris, Evan Davis, Charles Campell, subversivevids.com, buzznet.com, oaththreadline.com, worldsmosthated.com, ock1337, heychrission, Birdboys/Black Bunnies worldwide, Chicago FSU and the staff of the Chicago Elizabeth Arden Red Door Salon.